The BROWN WATER NAVY

The River and Coastal War in
Indo-China and Vietnam,
1948–1972

The BROWN WATER NAVY

The River and Coastal War in Indo-China and Vietnam, 1948–1972

Col. Victor Croizat USMC, Retd.

BLANDFORD PRESS
POOLE · DORSET

First published in the U.K. 1984 by Blandford Press,
Link House, West Street, Poole, Dorset, BH15 1LL

Copyright © 1984 Blandford Press Ltd.

Distributed in the United States by
Sterling Publishing Co., Inc.,
2 Park Avenue, New York, N.Y. 10016

British Library Cataloguing in Publication Data

Croizat, Victor J.
The brown water navy: warfare on the inland waters of
Southeast Asia.
1. Indochinese War, 1946-1954—Naval operations.
2. Vietnamese Conflict, 1961-1975—Naval operations.
3. Vietnam—History—1945-1975
I. Title
959.704   DS556.9

ISBN 0 7137 1272 4

Typeset by Asco Trade Typesetting Limited, Hong Kong
Printed in U.K. by BAS Printers Ltd., Wallop Hampshire

CONTENTS

Foreword

Armies fight on land, navies fight at sea; inland and coastal waters are obstacles to one and hazards to the other. These difficult areas, neither green like the land nor blue like the sea, are the domain of the brown water navy.

Amphibious forces are organized, equipped and trained to effect the orderly transition from sea to land combat. Because of this they can operate in brown waters. Yet, their primary concern, like that of the more conventional land and sea forces, is to overcome and transit rather than fight in that demanding and generally adverse environment. Thus, when extended operations are to be conducted in brown waters, the combat forces to be engaged and their equipment must be adapted to that purpose. Such was the experience of the French in the Indochina War and such was the experience of the Americans in the Vietnam War that followed.

It is our purpose here to review that experience as it was gained in the brown waters of the Indochinese Peninsula.

Acknowledgements

Much of the material used in this survey of brown water warfare was gathered in the course of several assignments in Southeast Asia that span the period 1954 to 1968. These involved active participation in the evacuation of North Vietnam (Haiphong, 1954), the Franco-American Military Training Mission, TRIM (Saigon, 1955–1956), the Fleet Marine Force, U.S. Seventh Fleet (Okinawa, 1960), the Southeast Asia Treaty Organization (Bangkok, 1961–64), the Fleet Marine Force, Pacific Riverine Warfare Study (South Vietnam, 1966) and the RAND office (Saigon, 1968).

Some of the data concerned have been used earlier in articles and studies appearing in other publications. Thus, in the United States, thanks are due, first, to the Rand Corporation in Santa Monica, California for permission to use RAND Memorandum RM 5271-PR of May 1967 entitled 'A Translation from the French: Lessons of the War in Indochina', Volume 2, and RAND paper 3616 of June 1967 entitled 'The Mekong River Development Project', and, second, to the US Naval Institute for permission to use 'The Origins of the Vietnamese Naval Forces' appearing in the Proceedings of February 1973, as source materials and for citation. Acknowledgement is equally due to the Office of Military History of the Department of the U.S. Army, for photographs and references, notably its two Vietnam studies entitled 'Riverine Operations 1966–1969' and 'Tactical and Material Innovations'. The Naval Historical Center of the Department of the U.S. Navy, the History and Museums Division of the U.S. Marine Corps and the *U.S. Marine Corps Gazette* have been equally generous in providing other data and photographs.

In France, the authorization granted to use the facilities and select photographs from the extensive files of the Musée de le Marine, Palais de Chaillot and the Division des Archives Audiovisuelles Militaires, Fort d'Ivry is gratefully appreciated. Equally welcome was the information provided by the Service Historique de l'Armée de Terre at the Chateau de Vincennes. Finally, recognition is due to General de Brigade Jean Louis Delayen, Infanterie de Marine, for his valued collaboration in the formation of the Vietnamese Marine Corps, assistance in the current endeavor, and the friendship that has endured throughout the intervening years.

The maps and other line illustrations were prepared by Design Post Associates of Bournemouth, England. Marks above the U.S. symbol for an infantry unit (a crossed rectangle) show its size: platoon, three dots; company, one line; battalion, two lines; regiment, nothing. Numerals on the right identify the regiment; those on the left, the battalion. Thus, 3···47 is one platoon 3 Bn 47th Rgt. A, B, and C are companies; RCN equals reconnaissance.

Abbreviations

APB	Barracks Ship (Self-Propelled)	LCM	Landing Craft, Mechanized	LSSL	Landing Ship, Support, Large
APL	Barracks Ship (Non-Self-Propelled)	LCP	Landing Craft, Personnel	LST	Landing Ship, Tank
		LCS	Landing Craft, Support	LVT	Landing, Vehicle, Tracked
ARL	Landing Craft Repair Ship	LCT	Landing Craft, Tank	MRB	Mobile River Base
ASPB	Assault Support Patrol Boat	LCU	Landing Craft, Utility	PACV	Patrol Aircushion Vehicles
ATC	Armored Troop Carrier	LCVP	Landing Craft, Vehicle, Personnel		
CCB	Command and Communications Boat	LSD	Landing Ship, Dock	PBR	River Patrol Boat
		LSI	Landing Ship, Infantry	PG	Patrol Gunboat
CGUB	Coast Guard Utility Boat	LSIL	Landing Ship, Infantry, Large	YMS	Auxiliary Minesweeper
LCA	Landing Craft, Armor	LSM	Landing Ship, Medium	YTB	Harbor Tug, Large
LCI	Landing Craft, Infantry			YTL	Auxiliary Tug, Small

PART 1
AN HISTORICAL PERSPECTIVE

1

Brown Water Warfare

The grandeur and endurance of ancient civilizations is related to the effectiveness with which they controlled and used their water resources. Inland and inshore waters were the first great avenues of movement and commerce; warfare on and from waterways has been the inevitable concomitant. This truism extends to the present day in Southeast Asia where the Mekong and Red River basins were the scene of combat operations by the brown water navies of France, Vietnam, and the United States. The historical and geographical notes that follow provide the background to those conflicts.

Man has long made use of the rivers, bays and inlets of the lands he occupied to better his agriculture and facilitate his commerce in peace and to move and support his military forces in war. He has flourished in the measure that he has learned to use them.

In Mesopotamia, land of the Tigris and Euphrates Rivers where the earliest urban communities appeared, the gain in importance of the south was paced to the development of irrigation. In Egypt, it was the Nile River that made the desert fruitful and provided the communications that enabled another ancient civilization to arise. This was an inward-looking conservative society, made so largely by the deserts that isolated it. Yet, the Nile opened the Mediterranean world to the Egyptians, who developed the trireme some eight centuries before Christ. This type of war vessel remained the standard model for several centuries.

Early records of organized warfare make many references to seapower, navies, and engagements afloat. Today such words refer mainly to blue water activities; in antiquity the reference was almost always limited to brown waters. In ancient Greece, land armies used water transport and were supported by combat fleets. There was little difference

between these components as combat fleets were not unlike waterborne infantry or cavalry and elements on the water were closely tied to events on land. Cooperation between elements ashore and afloat was invariably close since ships sailed near the shore and beached at night. Combat tactics afloat or ashore differed little and the roles of general and admiral, or soldier and marine, were interchangeable. The special skills required of the sailor were, however, acknowledged. The 225 men making up the crew of the standard Athenian trireme, some 45 meters long and six meters of beam, included 175 rowers and equal numbers of sailors and marines separately identified.

In 480 BC some 200 of these ships were assembled to meet a vastly more numerous Persian fleet manned by experienced Phoenician mercenary seamen. The Greeks, aware of their inferior

numbers and hastily trained crews, lured the Persian fleet into narrow waters where their numerical superiority was nullified. The Greek victory that followed at Salamis ended the threat of Persian domination and ranks as the western world's first decisive naval battle.

In the century to follow, the Greeks engaged in a succession of internal conflicts culminating in the establishment of Macedonian supremacy over the whole of Greece. In 336 BC Alexander became king. Two years later he crossed into Asia Minor to begin the campaign which, in 326, brought him to the Kingdom of Taxila in what is now northwest Pakistan. Soon thereafter, his troops refused to continue eastward. Alexander, bending to their will, returned to the Hydaspes River, now the Jhelum. There he built a fleet on which he embarked part of his force and, with the remainder paralleling the waterways along their

The first known reference to warships separately identified from other types of craft is attributed to the Egyptians thirty centuries before Christ. These were ships made of reeds, the most readily available boatbuilding material. A fleet of forty such ships reportedly sailed for Phoenicia in 2900 BC in quest of ship timbers. Fifteen centuries later Egyptian ships sail-

ing the Red Sea were of the type depicted. These in time evolved into the 24 meter long bireme which served as the leading warship type in the region into the eighth century BC. Thereafter they yielded preeminence to the triremes which carried the day for the Greeks at the famous naval battle of Salamis (480 BC).

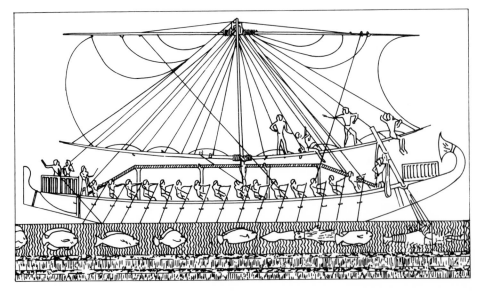

banks, he travelled downstream to the Indus River and thence to its delta. There, where Karachi now stands, he detached one of his generals, Nearchus, to embark part of his force and proceed westward by sea along the northern coast of the Arabian Sea and Persian Gulf while he, Alexander, moved overland with the main body. The two forces eventually were joined on the Amanis River, now the Dozdan, near the present-day Iranian town of Minab on the upper arc of the Strait of Hormuz. Nearchus left us an account of his voyage in sufficient detail to allow his passage to be traced. Little appears to have changed to this day along the desolate Makran coast of Baluchistan, today shared by Pakistan and Iran, that he identified as the 'land of the fish eaters'.

Rome entered history as a land power to whom waterways were an obstacle. This is affirmed by the historian Vegetius, who noted that every legion had an

The Nile flows through Cairo.

The Blue and White Niles meet near Khartoum, Sudan. The Nile, flowing over 6500 kilometers, is the longest river in the world. Its basin comprises one-tenth of the land area of Africa and supports over 50 million people. Its waters have been used for irriga-tion since the beginning of civilization, although the first modern works built for that purpose date only from 1843. The first Aswan Dam was started at the turn of the century. The new High Dam, 7 kilometers upstream, was completed in 1971.

River port of Minab where dhows, more often diesel powered today, come to load dates for shipment across the Persian Gulf. Dhows are the traditional working boats of southwestern Asia. Their name appears to derive from the Swahili word 'daw' meaning boat. There are more than 2500 dhows serving the ports of the Persian Gulf and Sea of Oman today. These range in length from 10 to 30 meters and in capacity from 5 to 350 tons. Their sails, still in use, are a modification of the lateen type found on the feluccas of the Nile. Dhows today carry cargos ranging from baskets of dates to television sets and even an occasional new Mercedes automobile.

engineer detachment with pontoons for bridging. He also related that the Romans preferred a site along the Tiber for recruit training since, among other skills, all legionnaires had to know how to swim. But water did not remain an alien element for long. When Rome completed the conquest of the Italian peninsula, it encountered the Carthaginians who ruled the western Mediterranean. If Roman interests in the south were to be safeguarded, the menace of Carthage had to be overcome. For this Rome turned to the sea.

In the First Punic War (265–241 BC), Rome gained Sicily and deprived Carthage of its superiority afloat. Carthage then decided that its best remaining course was to attack Rome by land. The Second Punic War began two decades after the First had ended with Carthaginian attacks on Roman colonies in Spain. From there, Hannibal and his armies fought their way along the Mediterranean to cross the Alps into Italy, where for the next fifteen years he conducted a campaign that numbered several brilliant victories but proved inconclusive. During these years the Romans used their recently acquired seapower to bring the war to Africa. Hannibal eventually was recalled to meet this threat, but by then Carthage was unable to hold and Hannibal met his final defeat at Zama in 202 BC.

Two generations later the Carthaginians again renewed the conflict, but this time the disparity of forces was too great. The Third Punic War lasted only four years and was concluded with the complete destruction of Carthage itself. Thus, Carthage and Rome reversed traditional roles. The maritime power took to the land, while the land power took to the sea to find victory in the wise use of the complementary advantages of land and sea forces.

The military might of Rome was in its disciplined infantry whose effectiveness on land also proved itself afloat when necessity made Rome a sea power. The successor East Roman Empire was a maritime state from the first. It owed its long endurance to the horse archer on land and a highly effective navy skillfully adapted to move and support its land forces and to fight in coastal waters. In the eighth century this capability was represented by an imperial fleet based at Constantinople and several provincial fleets based on the southern coast of Asia Minor, in Italy and Sicily, and on a number of Aegean islands.

The mainstay of the Byzantine navy was the 'droman' or 'racer'. This was a twin-banked, single-masted galley able to carry up to 300 men. The Byzantines had also developed revolving turrets, landing craft with ramps to permit the assault landing of mounted cavalry, and sea-borne flame throwers. The soundness of the naval organization, the excellence of its operations, and the innovativeness of its equipment all contributed to the success of the Byzantine navy. In six centuries it was challenged only twice.

The East Roman Empire eventually fragmented under Slav and Muslim attack. During this long process and at the end of the eighth century, Scandinavian peoples exploded over Europe. These were the Vikings whose raids along the coasts and incursions deep into the continental river systems encouraged the spread of feudalism as an effective countermeasure. The Viking ship was a double-ended, single-banked, single-masted vessel some 25 meters long and able to carry up to 200 men. It was exceptionally sea-worthy and its shallow draft allowed it to move easily through inland waters. It was not, however, a warship intended for combat afloat.

The Vikings moved by boat but fought ashore. They were both pirate and trader, sacking or settling as circumstances permitted. At first cautious in their early ninth century forays, they soon became bold enough to sack London, Cadiz, and Seville. They also laid siege to Paris and settled in sufficient numbers in France to be granted Normandy by the French king in AD 911. They reached into the Mediterranean, capturing cities in Italy and Morocco, and sailed west to Iceland, Greenland, and North America. Finally, in the east, they moved through the river systems of Russia. There they established Novgorod and Kiev, and by 865 they were besieging Constantinople. In 941 they led a Russian fleet to the Black Sea, where it was destroyed in an action with the Byzantine navy.

The depredations of the Vikings over three centuries were facilitated by the absence of local defense organizations and cohesive governments. In time, heavy cavalry demonstrated its ability to cope with these northmen and the people rediscovered the merits of fortified communities within which they could shelter. This had been well appreciated by the Byzantines who had covered their

The Columbia near its confluence with the Snake River. These two rivers, like the Mississippi and Missouri to the east, played an important part in the exploration and settlement of the western United States. The Columbia is the longest river flowing from North America to the Pacific Ocean. One third of its 1900 kilometers length is in Canada; the remainder flows through Washington and forms the boundary between that state and Oregon. The river once had many rapids but extensive works for irrigation and hydro-electric power have made it among the tamest rivers in the United States.

Danube River frontier with fifty-two fortresses upstream, backed by twenty-seven to the south. The feudal system that evolved, typified in England by the 1200 castles established within a century of the Norman invasion, gradually restored the stability of the countryside as raiding became less profitable. The decline of the Vikings that ensued was paralleled by the beginnings of true seapower.

The sea battle off Dover in 1217 marked the start of six centuries of intermittent war between the French and the English. It also stands as among the first examples of war at sea involving the maneuver of sailing ships. This development of sailing ships was to continue, particularly among Atlantic nations. In the Mediterranean the galley retained its dominance until the battle of Lepanto in 1571, when the Christian fleet overcame

that of the Turks. In that battle the superiority of the ship with deck mounted cannon over the traditional galley was violently demonstrated. The English then went on to discover that great guns able to sink ships were more effective than smaller guns intended principally to cause personnel casualties. This led to changes in ship design, leading in 1637 to the launching of the *Sovereign of the Seas*, a true battleship mounting one hundred great guns on three decks. Thus, the blue water navy appeared in the majesty of the sailing ships of the line that were to endure with little change until the age of steam.

Brown water operations were not long in reasserting their importance. This is clearly evident in the history of the United States, which is rich in examples of naval operations complementing those of land armies, particularly by forces operating on the rivers and lakes of the continent. Beginning with the War of Independence, brown water warfare has been a regular feature in early American military history. Control of Lake Champlain, Lake George, and the Hudson River was of primary importance in that first struggle. Then, in the War of 1812, the conflict extended over the Great Lakes and on to the river approaches to Washington and New Orleans. A generation later the Seminole Wars in Florida introduced the American Army, Navy, and Marines ·to brown water combat in an environment not unlike that of Southeast Asia.

In the American War of Independence the British effort to isolate New England led to a series of engagements afloat for the control of Lake Champlain, Lake George, and the Hudson River. In 1776 the Americans, forced out of Canada, fell back on Lake Champlain. Both sides then began to assemble a fleet to contest control of the lake. The British force of some thirty vessels, including several schooners, was under navy command. The smaller American force that included eight specially built gondolas was under command of an army officer, Benedict Arnold, who decided to sortie and challenge the British before their preparations were completed. In the running engagement that followed the Americans were defeated. They nonetheless had succeeded in delaying the southward advance of the British for one year. This was critical, for by 1777 the Americans had become strong enough to win the battle of Saratoga and the French had entered the war.

The War of 1812 was even more striking in the importance of the inland maritime operations. Again, in the north, the British and Americans raced to build fleets to gain control of Lake Erie. The American Commodore Oliver Perry overcame an initial numerical advantage of the British Commodore Barclay and in September 1813 defeated the British in a bloody fight. His victory enabled the Americans to extend their control over the Great Lakes and helped assure their claim to the Northwest Territory.

In 1814, the reinforced British directed their energies toward New Orleans and Washington, and in a drive south from Canada. The last was halted on Lake Champlain in September by Macdonough's victory at Plattsburg. The other two drives were more difficult to counter, however, for they were based on British naval power which the Americans could in no way match. The defense of Washington depended largely upon the control of the river approaches. This task fell to Commodore Joshua Barney who had spent the winter of 1813 in building

and training a river flotilla. With the coming of spring, Barney began his campaign of harassment. A succession of engagements followed against British forces of ever increasing strength. Finally, in August, Barney was forced to destroy his boats to avoid capture and the British were free to move on to the capital which they burned on the 24 August.

The defense of New Orleans, like that of Washington, depended on control of the water approaches. An initial action on Lake Borgne resulted in the Americans being overwhelmed by a greatly superior British armada; they did nonetheless gain time for General Jackson to prepare the defenses of the city. Subsequently, the energetic actions of General Jackson and Commodore Patterson kept the British off balance and eventually denied them final victory.

A generation later United States forces again faced combat in a riverine environment; this time in an area and under circumstances close to those that were to test them 130 years later in Southeast

Commodore Perry's expedition in the treacherous Devil's Turn of the Tabasco River. The war with Mexico in 1848 provided yet another occasion for the U.S. Navy to demonstrate its ability to adapt blue water resources to brown water requirements. The passage of the Devil's Turn downriver from Fort Iturbide covering the town of San Juan Bautista was a classic example of a riverine force using its embarked infantry to land and drive off an enemy seeking to deny further movement on an inland waterway. (USN)

Asia. The Seminole War had its origins in the refusal of the Florida Indians to comply with the Indian Removal Act and relocate on reservations in the west. Hostilities began in 1835 with an Indian attack on an army detachment near Tampa. The navy was called in to keep the Chatahoochie River open for the movement of supplies and for operations against the Indians. This initial mission was eventually expanded to require a force of over 600 soldiers, sailors, and marines and 150 assorted craft. These last ranged from flat-bottomed boats used to penetrate the Everglades to three schooners used to patrol along the coastal inlets.

In the war with Mexico the U.S. Navy varied its routine blockade duties by twice assaulting the town of San Juan Bautista some seventy miles upriver from the port of Frontera. The first raid, in October 1846, encountered light resistance and was speedily accomplished. But after the Americans withdrew, the movement of contraband through the area was resumed and a second punitive expedition was required. For this purpose, the U.S. Navy organized a naval brigade of 2500 men embarked in ten ships and numerous boats. The force set forth on 14 June and encountered obstacles well covered by fire at a difficult bend, the Devil's Turn. The brigade was landed to rout the defenders while the boats and ships cleared the obstacles. The force

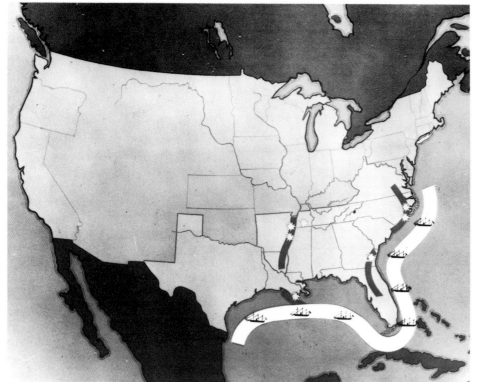

The Union blockade of the South during the American Civil War and the principal brown water combats. (USN)

then moved on to Fort Iturbide, the last defensive position just below the city, where the position was again overcome by the combined action of forces ashore and afloat.

The dramatic exploits of Lee's lieutenants have stimulated widespread interest in the land campaigns of the American Civil War. This has tended to overshadow the contribution of the navy to its final outcome. The importance of naval operations during this war becomes readily apparent on a map, where the Confederacy is seen to have consisted largely of a coastal plain and piedmont. The navy's blockade of the coast and its penetration of the Mississippi River basin thus helped to isolate the Confederacy and at the same time brought the navy into position to support the Union Army directly. Here it may be noted that the Civil War officially began with a brown water incident when a naval force sought to resupply Fort Sumter, built on a shoal at the entrance to Charleston harbor. Equally noteworthy is that the naval strategy of the Union was announced shortly after the fall of Fort Sumter by the aged General-in-Chief of the Army, Winfield Scott.

River operations were centered initially at Cairo, Illinois where Commander Rogers converted three river steamers into unarmored gunboats. His successor, Flag Officer Foote, added seven armored 13-gun boats that greatly extended the navy's capabilities. As these craft came into service they were quickly engaged in patrolling, troop transport, supply support, raiding, and related tasks to deny the Confederates the use of waterways and prevent the secession of Kentucky and Missouri. The ironclads in particular enabled Foote to join with General Grant's forces in an attack on Fort Henry to open the Tennessee River. Shortly thereafter, on 16 February 1862, the Union forces seized Fort Donelson and opened the way to Nashville. Columbus fell to Foote's gunboats on 4 March and on 6 April gunboat fire turned the tide of victory in Grant's favor at Shiloh. At almost the same time, a Confederate

Commodore Foote's riverine assault on Fort Henry, Tennessee River. The rôle of the U.S. Navy in the Civil War is over-shadowed by the land campaigns of the Confederacy under General Lee and those of the Union forces under General Grant. Nonetheless, the blockade of Confederate ports and the penetration of

U.S. naval forces into the Mississippi River basin were of major importance in deciding the outcome of the war. Commodore Foote's armored 13-gun river boats provided the support needed for the attack on Fort Henry, whose capture opened the Tennessee River to Union forces. (USN)

Gunboats and mortar boats bombarding Island No. 10, the 'key' to the Mississippi. The loss of Fort Donelson that followed the capture of Fort Henry caused the Confederates to abandon their positions in Kentucky and retreat to Island No. 10 on the Mississippi. Two months later this bastion too was reduced with comparatively little effort by yet another riverine force. These and subsequent operations on inland waters divided the Confederacy which, already isolated by the coastal blockade and unable to import the essentials of war, eventually succumbed. (USN)

stronghold on the Mississippi, Island Number 10, was overwhelmed.

While these operations were proceeding in the north, Admiral Farragut moved heavy ships into the mouth of the Mississippi. He then forced a passage past Fort Jackson and Fort St Philips, and on 25 April anchored at New Orleans, thereby gaining the south's wealthiest city. The northern units, under Captain C.H. Davis since May of that year, meanwhile continued south to occupy Fort Pillow on 4 June and Memphis two days later; they met Farragut's flotilla above Vicksburg later. This city, which could have been taken easily early in 1862, had recently built defenses and was able to hold out for another year; it did not surrender until 4 June 1863.

During the nineteenth century, while the United States was asserting its independence and evolving into a major world power, the rivers of Africa were being used to open the interior of the continent to exploration. Early in the century a Scotsman, Mungo Park, estab-

lished the general course of the Niger River and, in 1828, René Caille of France reached Timbuctu. Later, Brazza, Stanley and Livingstone were to penetrate deep into the Congo River basin and settle the question of whether or not the Congo and Nile both arose from a single lake in the center of the continent. Then, in 1897, Kitchener with 25,000 men invaded Sudan by moving upriver to Omdurman where the Blue and White Niles meet. There he defeated a Mahdist host of 60,000 and extended British control over the upper reaches of the river upon which Egypt depended for its survival. The nineteenth century also marked the formal establishment of the French in Indochina.

This historical overview illustrates the importance that brown waters have had on social, economic, and political activities since earliest times. The economic importance is manifest in the continuous efforts made to improve, extend, or utilize water resources more effectively. The social and political significance is exemplified in the Byzantine navy and in the influence of the Viking incursions on the growth of feudalism.

The record of history further reveals that brown water navies existed well before the Christian era. These were conceived to support land armies. They invariably operated in close collaboration with forces ashore and when engaged afloat used tactics similar to those of

ground formations. These two qualities, the close collaboration between forces afloat and ashore and the similarity of their tactics, represent two fundamental characteristics of brown water warfare.

A third characteristic of brown water warfare is the exceptional innovativeness required of forces afloat. This is apparent in the navy of the early Romans which refined ram tactics and made highly effective use of disciplined, embarked infantry; in the Byzantine navy which used archers and flamethrowing devices and had landing craft for cavalry; and in the American Union navy which first used steam vessels, monitors and such specialized craft for combat on inland waters.

Blue water navies first appeared less than five hundred years ago when the improvement in sailing vessels enabled navies to operate well out at sea where they could devise purely naval tactics. Thus, naval warfare emerged as distinctly separate from ground warfare, and brown water navies, as such, virtually disappeared. But, as the evidence affirms, blue water navies have time and again been called upon to revert to earlier concepts of operations in inland and inshore waters. This was true in the War of 1812 and even more so in the American Civil War where the most significant contribution of the U.S. Navy was in the coastal blockade and riverine warfare tasks it so effectively accomplished.

In modern terms, the role of naval forces at sea or in amphibious operations from the sea is well understood. This is a familiar naval environment where established doctrine applies. However, when naval forces penetrate inland or close to shore, as they did in Indochina, their rôle becomes complementary to that of land forces. They must then regain the traditional character of their brown water antecedents of long ago.

The wars in Indochina confirmed that the brown water environment is an integral part of the land environment. The freedom of action which naval forces enjoy at sea is severely restricted when they move inland. Currents, obstacles, variable depths of water, and unreliable charts all make for difficult navigation. High river banks, dense vegetation, and the convolutions of the terrain reduce visibility and the effectiveness of flat

A cannon port in a Royal ceremonial galley of the Thai Navy. These galleys, built on lines common to the river navies of Southeast Asian countries, are used by the Thais in an annual naval parade.

Above right
A cannon port in the bow of a river navy galley.

Right
A Royal Thai Navy war galley.

trajectory weapons with which seagoing ships and craft are normally armed. The meanders of waterways and the presence of islands and shoals confine movement to channels that can easily be mined or where hostile fire can be brought to bear at short range.

The effect of these conditions is that naval vessels required to operate on brown waters need to be specially configured for the purpose. They also need to adhere to tactical procedures similar to those of ground forces. If the mission, for example, is the resupply of a river post in an insecure zone, the movement afloat must be made in convoy like that of a truck column on the road. If the mission is operational such as in a movement to contact the enemy, the force afloat will need armament and protection similiar to that of a mechanized formation prepared for imminent ground combat.

In summary, the two traditional characteristics of brown water warfare involving the close collaboration of forces afloat and ashore and the adaptation of ground force tactics by the forces afloat remain valid. Equally valid is the importance placed upon innovativeness as a quality essential to a brown water navy. All of these qualities were demonstrated repeatedly in the French, Vietnamese, and American experiences in Southeast Asia.

17

2
Indo-China Overview

Rivers are the lifelines of continents. They open new lands to settlement, serve as roadways, support fisheries, extend agriculture and provide power. Their importance is economic, political and social.

The relationship of man and brown waters is nowhere as evident as it is in Asia. There, the intensity of the traffic and the sprawl of sampan communities give waterways a color and dynamism unlike those of other regions. In China, the incredible Yangtze River, 5500 kilometers long, offers 4500 kilometers of navigable waters. Large cargo ships can reach 1000 kilometers upriver; smaller ships can continue for 2000 kilometers more. To add further dimension, the Imperial Canal, started in the fifth century BC, now allows river craft of up to 2000 tons to travel the 1700 kilometers from near the mouth of the Yangtze to Peking. All this explains why, before World War II, the United States had organized the Yangtze River Patrol and had operated it over some 2500 kilometers of the river to safeguard American lives and property in China. At the other end of the scale is the Kwae River of Thailand used to transport some of the prisoners and much of the material required by the Japanese army to build the notorious Thai-Burma railway in 1942–3, which was intended to support Japanese operations in Burma.

The rivers of Indochina fall between these extremes. Like the Yangtze they are the vital arteries of the land; like the Kwae they are silent witnesses to much human misery.

The term Indochina relates to a political entity created by the French at the end of the nineteenth century. It included the Kingdoms of Laos and Cambodia plus the territories of Cochinchina, Annam and Tonkin now reunited as Vietnam. Indochina also identifies the easternmost part of peninsular Southeast Asia, a geographic region that shares the Mekong River and has been the interface

Above
Junks off the coast of Vietnam.

Below
The Mekong at Chiang Saen where the Thai, Lao and Burma borders meet. The Mekong River, which empties into the South China Sea some 4000 kilo-

meters from its source in Tibet, has marked a zone of interaction between Indian and Chinese cultures for centuries. Before it branches below Phnom Penh, its minimum flow is twice that of the Columbia at its mouth. Its vast delta, which forms much of Cochinchina, was the scene of brown water combats during the Indochina and Vietnam Wars.

The Saigon to Mytho rail line was the first built in Indochina. Started in 1884, its 71 kilometer run was completed in 1885.

The course of the Mekong River itself is only some 250 kilometers in South Vietnam, but the navigable waterways in the delta area extend over 3900 kilometers. Of this total, some 1290 kilometers are canals with a mean depth of 2 meters at low water. The remainder are natural or improved waterways radiating outward from the Mekong, the Vaico, Dong Nai and Saigon Rivers. The French began mechanical dredging in 1893 and are largely responsible for the development of the deltaic area. They also encouraged early Vietnamese migration into the area to relieve population pressures in the north and extend the agricultural base of the south.

zone between Indian and Chinese cultures since the beginning of recorded history. The Mekong is the principal river of Laos and Cambodia. Its delta forms Cochinchina, the southern part of Vietnam. This is linked by the narrow mountain-backed coastal plain of Annam to the Red River delta in north Vietnam, formerly Tonkin.

More than a thousand years ago a poet wrote of a lofty pure land that was the center of snow mountains and the source of great rivers. This is an apt description of Tibet, a remote and sparsely populated country of physical superlatives. Tibet is a vast wind-swept plateau, much of it lying above 5000 meters. It is walled off from the south by the highest mountains on earth, the Himalayas, and is elsewhere enclosed by ramparts difficult to penetrate. In the east, however, the compressed relief abruptly adopts a southerly trend that gradually opens toward the south — like a fan — to become the peninsula of Southeast Asia.

Within the base of the fan, the Yangtze, Mekong and Salween Rivers flow in deep parallel valleys within 100 kilometers of one another. Then the Yangtze takes up an eccentric northeasterly course to flow through Yunnan, past Chungking, and across the Tunting Lake plain to reach the China Sea near Shanghai. The Salween continues to flow south and remains confined for its 3000 kilometer run

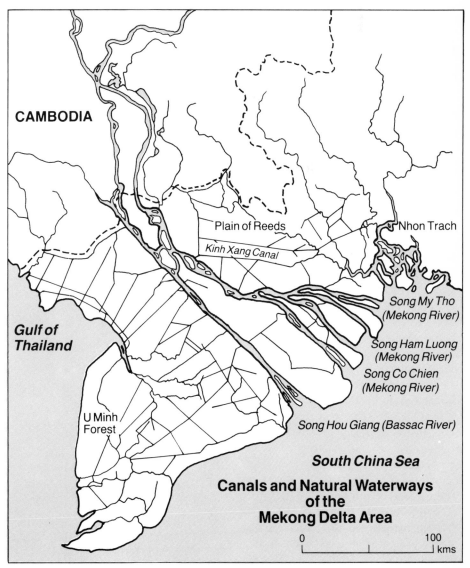

CAMBODIA

Plain of Reeds

Kinh Xang Canal

Nhon Trach

Song My Tho (Mekong River)

Gulf of Thailand

Song Ham Luong (Mekong River)

Song Co Chien (Mekong River)

U Minh Forest

Song Hou Giang (Bassac River)

South China Sea

Canals and Natural Waterways of the Mekong Delta Area

0   100

kms

to the Gulf of Martaban near Moulmein. The Mekong also flows south at first, but then it is progressively deflected eastward to make its way to the South China Sea below Saigon.

For the first third of its 4000 kilometer course, the Mekong River flows from Tibet through China under the name Lan Tsang. It takes the name Mekong when it reaches Burma, where it briefly forms the boundary between that country and China. The Mekong then turns east to flow past Luang Prabang, ancient capital of the three-headed elephant Kingdom of Laos, where it again turns south to emerge as the boundary between Laos and Thailand.

From Vientiane, present capital of Laos, to Savannakhet the Mekong is navigable, but below Savannakhet it cuts through a sandstone plateau which gives rise to the Khemmarat rapids. These make navigation difficult and, when the river again enters Laos shortly thereafter, it reaches the Khone Falls where it becomes impassable. During the Indochina War the French maintained a military truck service to supplement the seven kilometer long railway that had been built years before as a bypass.

A few kilometers below the falls the Mekong enters Cambodia, where it is turned eastwards by the Cardamom Mountains. In prehistoric times the sea reached deep into Cambodia to form the Tonle Sap or Great Lake. Then, as the Mekong built its first delta, the Tonle Sap was cut off from the sea. It thenceforth received its waters from the Mekong, as it does today. Now the Great Lake regulates the flow of the Mekong by storing its waters during the flood season and returning them during the dry period. In this fashion, the Tonle Sap helps maintain the productivity of the land; it also yields enormous quantities of fish each year. Phnom Penh, the capital of Cambodia, now Kampuchea, lies where the Mekong shares its waters with the Great Lake. At that point, the minimum flow of the Mekong River is twice that of the Columbia at its mouth on America's northwest Pacific coast.

Upon passing Phnom Penh, the Mekong divides into two branches and enters Vietnam. There it further divides as it makes its way across a monotonous alluvial plain. The sea once extended undisturbed from the foothills of the Annam Cordillera, the mountains of Vietnam in the east, to the Cardamom mountains of Cambodia in the west. In time, this vast area was filled with rich alluvium from the Mekong River. The 13,000 sq. km. basin thus formed, today still lies at an elevation of less that three meters above sea level. However, it is continuing to grow at the rate of 60 to 80 meters a year as a result of the 800 million cubic meters of new alluvium the river deposits each year.

The drainages of the Dong Nai, Saigon, and Vaico Rivers in the east, that flow above and below Saigon, constitute an area of limited fertility. However, it was found that rubber would grow well there. A first plantation was started in 1924 and by 1938 there were 98,000 hectares (242,000 acres) of rubber planta-

Charcoal makers in a Rung Sat village. The Rung Sat, which in Vietnamese means 'dense jungle', is a vast mangrove swamp lying between Saigon and the sea. Much of the area is difficult to penetrate because of its lacing waterways and the density of the mangrove that covers some 85 per cent. of the area. Villages, used principally by charcoal makers who help to supply Saigon with this basic fuel, have been established in the open areas. The communists used the area as a transit zone between the U.S. III and IV Corps areas and set up supply depots and other facilities. In 1964, the area was declared a 'Special Zone' and was assigned to the Vietnamese Navy as its only territorial command.

tion in the area. The nearby Plain of Reeds, covering some 7000 sq. kms. (5300 sq. kms. in Vietnam) is poorly drained and of low fertility.

The Mekong delta itself is rich throughout its expanse although in its southern extremity near Ca Mau the land is still too new to yield much beyond mangrove. Before these lands could be made to yield rice in abundance, they had to be drained and cleared. This process, laboriously begun by the Vietnamese, and the Cambodians before them, was greatly accelerated by the French.

The French made a sustained effort to improve the utility of this vast delta, which seldom rises above three meters in elevation, by dredging and canalization. The volume of dredged materials, which reached 140,000 cubic meters in 1893, fluctuated between six and ten million cubic meters annually between 1913 and 1930. This helped to create some 1200 kilometers of canals with a minimum depth of two meters to add to the 2700 kilometers of other waterways; it also greatly increased the area of lands available for cultivation. In the first fifty years of French administration the area of available ricelands in Cochinchina quadrupled to reach 2.2 million hectares, this richness and accessibility attracting large populations. It is for these reasons that

20

Spur of the Annam Cordillera reaching the sea to compartment the beaches along the coast of Annam.

Above right
Land communications across the narrow waterways of Annam were vulnerable to enemy action. When destroyed, bridges were most easily replaced by pontoon causeways.

The 'Mountains of Marble' rise from the coastal plain near Danang.

control of the Mekong delta was a primary objective in both the Indochina and Vietnam Wars.

To the north of the Mekong delta, the narrow waist of Annam consists of a coastal plain intermittently fronted by sand dunes and backed by the Annam Cordillera or Chaine Annamitique. These highlands are eroded plateaux whose steep eastern slopes descend in spurs that compartment the lowlands and occasionally plunge directly into the sea. The highlands also give rise to the short, swift rivers that water the coastal plain and provide it with some 3000 kilometers of useable waterways. Their navigability, however, is impaired by shifting sand bars and uncertain water levels that vary widely. The rivers of central Annam all flow into lagoons that facilitate lateral movement. But, in the aggregate, there is no system of interconnected waterways as there is in either Cochinchina or

Tonkin. This dispersed aspect of the waterways of Annam lessens their regional importance but they remain most important locally. In Annam, as elsewhere in Southeast Asia, the majority of the people live on or near the waterways, which are the focus of economic activity.

The Tonkin delta of north Vietnam is an unusually level alluvial plain, of some 15,000 square kilometers, half lying below three meters in elevation. The plain is backed by steep mountains, abrupt and rugged, even as they first rise from the

plain. It has been formed by several rivers but takes its name from the Red River, which receives the waters of the Black and Clear Rivers just above the capital, Hanoi. The Red River rises in south China and flows some 1250 kilometers to empty into the Gulf of Tonkin. Its lower reaches link with other waterways to help form a network that extends over 3200 kilometers. The Red River delta, one of the most densely populated areas of Indochina, relies on rice cultivation.

As in Annam, navigability in the

The Baie d'Along, named 'Rock City' by American sailors, is characterized by numerous shafts of limestone projecting up from the sea, some to a height of 150 meters. On the west of the bay lies Cat Ba, the largest island in the area, on its south lies the lesser island of Apowan. The port of Haiphong lies on the Cua Cam some 15 kilometers from the sea, and is approached by a channel with a depth of six meters. U.S. Navy transports engaged in the evacutation of North Vietnam in 1954 drew too much water and were normally anchored in the Baie d'Along awaiting their loads of refugess shuttled to them on French Navy landing boats and ships.

Apowan fishing fleet. Apowan, in the Baie d'Along, shelters a small community of fishermen and boat builders. The French Navy maintained a small station on Apowan up to 1954.

Apowan Island: hull repairs are effected with hand-tools alone.

Tonkin: A boy tends his buffalo while rice grows green in the background. Rice cultivation, the most common economic activity of Tonkin, depends upon the successful control of river floods, accomplished by natural and artificial embankments. Despite modern measures, rice cultivation remains labor intensive and flooding a problem. After the rice is harvested, the grains are separated by beating them behind a wicker shield. The rice is bagged in the field, then loaded on a cart drawn by the ubiquitous water buffalo.

Tonkin delta is affected by extreme variations in water level. At Hanoi, for example, the flow of the Red River at high water equals the maximum discharge of the Danube, or twice that of the Nile. This flow, coupled with the level aspect of the terrain makes flooding a serious problem. Centuries ago this led to the building of dikes which eventually reached 15 meters in width. Under French administration, the dike system was extended to cover more than 2750 kilometers. The main dikes were widened to 50 meters and, near Hanoi, raised to as much as 13 meters. In addition to control of flooding, this expanded the delta's useable ricelands to where the pre-World War II production equalled one third of Indochina's total output on only a quarter of its cultivated area. This enabled the support of populations whose density, exceeding 800 per square kilometer, was among the world's highest.

In the decade before World War II, Tonkin had a population approaching nine million living on rice produced on 1.1 million hectares of cultivated land. This ratio was essentially the same in Annam (5.6 million people and 800,000 hectares of cultivated land) where population densities of 300 per square kilometer were still significant, although well below those of the north. In both regions the ricelands yielded two crops, and sometimes three in southern Annam, each year. Still, there was always hunger in poor crop years. The precarious balance between people and rice was further upset by medical services that reduced infant mortality. The resulting population pressures made movement out of these regions necessary and inevitable.

The Vietnamese, so their traditions state, were attracted neither to the mountains nor the sea. Only rice lands were the prize to be sought. Yet, in happier times, some 300,000 Vietnamese settled on the coast between the Red River delta and the Col des Nuages (Hai Van Pass north of Danang) and made their living as fishermen; this is attested by the richness of their language in nautical terms. Records also reveal that toward the end of the seventeenth century, when the Vietnamese were engaged in driving the Cambodians out of Cochinchina, the Vietnamese river fleet numbered 133 galleys. In the latter part of the following century, Nguyen Anh, legitimate heir to the throne of Cochinchina, set out to reunite the country. After seizing Hue and Hanoi, he proclaimed himself emperor in 1802 under the dynastic name of Gia Long. Among his subsequent accomplishments was the creation of the largest navy the country had ever had. This was made up of 500 medium galleys, each manned by 40 rowers and mounting one cannon and several mangonels (stone throwing engines). There were also 100 large galleys, each with as many as 70 rowers and several cannons and mangonels; 200 other craft, each armed with sixteen to 22 cannons; and three European ships. The British, who were not unknowing in such matters, thought the Vietnamese among the best seamen and boatbuilders in the Indies.

The expansion of the Vietnamese southward had begun at the end of the seventeenth century with the gradual destruction of the Chams along the coast and the ejection of the Cambodians from the Mekong delta. This movement had been encouraged further by the French who, beginning in 1888, introduced a number of resettlement programs that met with varying success. Efforts to settle Vietnamese inland ran afoul of malaria in the highlands. Further, the few fertile valleys were usually already occupied by mountain tribes of different ethnic origins who were less than welcoming. The opening of rubber plantations in Cochinchina did, however, attract Tonkinese labor, as did the new lands being opened to cultivation by dredging operations.

Eventually, on the eve of World War II there were some 4.6 million people settled in the south. This represented half the population of the north, enjoying the yield from twice the area so laboriously cultivated in Tonkin. Unlike Tonkin and Annam where two crops were wrested from the land each year, Cochinchina needed only one.

The data since then are uncertain, but it is clear that there has been significant further growth in the population of the south. The evacuation of Catholic and other refugees from the north to the south following upon the Geneva Accords of 1954 alone involved more than 750,000 people. In any event, the population of the south today has undoubtedly reached the level and density of that of Tonkin before World War II.

During the eighteenth century the Empire of Annam had been divided into Tonkin and Cochinchina. Cambodia at that time extended over the whole of the Mekong River delta and Laos occupied lands on both sides of the river. As the century advanced, the Vietnamese filtered south and west. The French appeared at the same time as traders and missionaries. They were tolerated at first, but as their numbers and influence increased their presence became less and less acceptable. This situation changed significantly in the century that followed.

In the course of the dynastic struggles that fragmented Annam, a French priest, Pigneau de Behaine, came to sponsor the Nguyen heir to Cochinchina, for whom he gained the support of Louis XVI. This proved decisive and by 1802 the French had helped in the seizure of Hue and Hanoi and in the accession of Gia Long as Emperor of Annam.

This assured the French of a favored position in the country throughout his lifetime, but, after his death in 1820, his heirs were not as well disposed. The French gradually lost favor and the situation deteriorated to the point where they had to use military force to protect their interests. In 1859, the French had seized Saigon, and three years later the Vietnamese ceded them part of Cochinchina.

A rubber plantation at tapping time, Ben Cat area, north of Saigon, 1955. Refugees from North Vietnam were settled in this area from 1954–55.

The Cambodian city of Angkor was founded by King Indravarma in the eighth century. The city served as a religious and political center and as a major component of a huge water resources control system. It was sacked four times in the fourteenth and fifteenth centuries by the Thais, after which it was abandoned to the jungle.

The remainder followed in 1867.

In the twelfth century the Kingdom of Cambodia included most of present day Thailand and all of Cochinchina. Thereafter the kingdom was progressively reduced by the Thais from the west and the Vietnamese from the east. The process was arrested by the French who, having taken Saigon in 1859, offered a protectorate to the King of Cambodia in 1863. He accepted rather than succumb to Thai designs on his Sovereignty. The Thais were placated over this intrusion by being given two provinces of western Cambodia, which were latter retaken by the French. On the Vietnam side, the border remained stable and Vietnamese expansion appeared to be checked.

French control over Cochinchina and Cambodia influenced Napoleon III to authorize the exploration of the Mekong River. The French were well aware of the commercial importance of the Yangtze and wanted to determine whether the Mekong could provide access to China's vast waterway system. Accordingly, in June 1866, an expedition under Doudart de Lagree set forth up the Mekong to ascertain the extent of its navigability. After two years of hardship and disappointments the French finally reached the Yangtze, but only by land; they had been defeated by the falls and rapids which made commercial navigation impossible in the upper reaches of the Mekong. They then shifted their interest to Tonkin as an alternate commercial gateway to China.

French traders were already using the Red River as a trade route. To protect these interests, Francis Garnier attacked and seized Hanoi in 1873. Garnier had accompanied Lagree up the Mekong and typified the dynamic empire builders of that century. His death at the hands of piratical Black Flag elements, coupled with the violence in the north decided the French administration in Saigon to seek use of the Red River through diplomatic rather than military means. But, while a

A Cambodian village chief and local villagers.

treaty to that end was signed in 1874, the continuing hostility of the Black Flags made it impossible to implement. The French moved in with military force and by 1884 they had established a protectorate over Tonkin. They then took over lands on the left bank of the Mekong to deny them to the Thais. These events were formalized in 1893 by the protectorate over Laos.

The French not only created the political entity of Indochina but also greatly influenced native living patterns. It is noteworthy that many of these changes were brought about by improvements in the utilization and management of water resources, notably those of the Mekong and Red River systems.

25

3
Origins of the Conflict

During the period of conquest and early colonization, French military rule over the lands being acquired inevitably lessened the rôle of the native systems of government. At the same time, there was little cooperation among the political entities in Indochina and little financial support from France. The appointment of civil governors helped to restore the functions of indigenous administrators. The problems of coordination and financial support were addressed by the creation in 1899 of the Indochinese Union as a political federation with its own budget.

By the beginning of the twentieth century the French had created a unified country under a governor general wherein stability and security prevailed. But, at the end of the Russo-Japanese War of 1905 there were signs of disaffection with French rule attributed to the European loss of face following upon the Russian defeat. This incipient unrest was aggravated by the exposure of some 140,000 Vietnamese to European political processes during service with the military in World War I. Their experience in Europe inspired formation of independence movements which were further strengthened by the French educational system that had been established in Indochina.

The Chinese Revolution and the rise of the Kuomintang in 1920 gave further impetus to Vietnamese nationalist movements. These, centered in Tonkin and Cochinchina, continued to grow to where in 1930 and 1931 they erupted into violence. The disturbances, although serious, were quelled by the French whose authority was never jeopardized. However, the situation did not endure long for the start of World War II in 1939 brought to French Indochina an era of uncertainty and conflict that has yet to end.

The first Japanese moves toward Indochina were made in early 1939 when troops landed on Hainan and the Spratly Islands. These actions were accompanied by increased pressure on French and British concessions in China and by restrictions on shipping in the South China Sea. In response to these events, the French reinforced their garrison in Indochina from 27,000 to 50,000 men. This was relatively insignificant, since the naval and air units remained small and their equipment remained outdated. Moreover, with the outbreak of the war in Europe, the possibility of receiving further support from France disappeared and Indochina was left to depend entirely on its own resources.

By the summer of 1940 the Japanese controlled the coast of China. At the same time, the British, hard pressed by the German victories on the European continent, accepted the Japanese request to close the Burma road. The only access to beleaguered China then remaining was the rail line from the Vietnamese port of Haiphong. But, this too, the Japanese would soon deny.

Whatever discretion the Japanese had used in their earlier dealings with the French was cast aside at the news that France had capitulated to the Germans. No sooner had the French ceased their resistance in Europe than the Japanese demanded that the railroad to Yunnan be closed to movements of war material to China and that they be allowed to station a control commission in the area. The Vichy Government could do little but agree, even though they suspected that this would only lead to more demands. These indeed followed promptly; on 1 August 1940 the Japanese presented the French a note requesting the right of transit for their troops across Tonkin, and the right to construct airfields in the country. They also imposed agreements intended to bind Indochina closely to Japanese economic interests.

Vichy informed the United States of these developments and pointed out that their ability to resist was directly related to the support that the United States could provide. The United States had placed an embargo upon shipment of high-grade steel, iron scrap and aviation gas to Japan on 26 July but was not in a position to provide direct military assistance to the French in Indochina. The French, unable to receive outside help, sought to prolong their negotiations with the Japanese. The outcome, however, was inevitable and the French were soon forced to grant the Japanese a number of concessions.

These were significant but less than what the Japanese had demanded at first. By terms of an agreement of 22 September 1940, the Japanese were given the use of three airfields in Tonkin, permission to station 6000 troops in the area, and the authority to move no more than 25,000 troops through Tonkin to Yunnan. It was also agreed that the Japanese could evacuate one division from south China through Tonkin.

Meanwhile, in the United States there were serious doubts over the effectiveness of the 26 July embargo, largely because it applied only to special items. During the month of August 1940, for example, licenses were granted for the export to

Japan of $21 million of petroleum products and 300,000 tons of steel and iron scrap. Thus, by the time the Japanese began to move into Tonkin, the United States was ready to extend its embargo to cover all types of iron and steel scrap. Oil was not included in the extension, even though there were advocates in the United States government for doing so.

Opponents of placing an embargo on oil shipments, which included the British, Dutch and Australians, based their position on the conviction that if Japan were to be denied United States oil, it would seek it elsewhere and probably attack the Dutch East Indies. The merits of this thesis cannot be debated with assurance but, when an embargo on oil was im-

Government and naval waterfront facilities, Saigon. The first port of Indochina, Saigon lies on the right bank of the river bearing the same name some 80 kilometres from the sea. Under the French, it handled the bulk of the traffic of southern Indochina and served as the main distribution center for the cargoes carried on the Mekong River. The port was opened to international traffic in 1861, two years after its capture. At that time it was little more than an agglomeration of villages living off the river trade, but the French began to build commercial facilities in 1865. The five-kilometer frontage of the port was divided by the Arroyo Chinois; to the north were the naval dock-yards, to the south the commercial area.

Left
Saigon City Hall. Saigon itself was laid out in a generally rectilinear pattern. The principal development of Saigon did not take place until the turn of the century. Much of the improvement was made necessary by the economic activity that followed the French settlement of the delta. During World War II, Saigon served as the main supply base for the Japanese forces stationed in southern Indochina. Later, the French used it as their administrative center and as the headquarters of their joint services command.

The Col de Blao on the Saigon-Dalat road was a good place for ambushes and any accident was certain to block traffic for hours. Communications throughout the Southern Highlands remain poor. The paved Saigon-Dalat road proceeds to the coast at Phan Rang. And an all-weather road reaches north from Saigon to parallel the east bank of the Mekong River, but only at Savannakhet is there an all-weather road link to the coast at Quang Tri. Kontum is linked to the coast but not to the river by a main road. Elsewhere, the quality of the roads is poor. The Americans did much to improve this road network but the quality of these improvements today is uncertain. The communists, denied the use of the coastal road and offshore waters by the Americans, turned to the uplands to establish their main supply route. The Ho Chi Minh trail complex followed the western slope of the highlands to the east of the Mekong River road developed by the French.

posed a year later, it coincided with the hardening of positions that soon led to war.

Thailand, meanwhile, looked upon these events as providing an opportunity to regain territories that had been ceded to the French by the treaties of 1893 and 1907. Accordingly, Thai forces began a series of probing attacks along the Cambodian border. By December 1940, fighting was general along much of the frontier and the French were being pressed hard. To ease the situation, the French moved a naval force into the Gulf of Thailand to seek out the Thai fleet. When the two forces met near the Koh

Chang Islands on 17 January 1941, the Thais suffered a decisive defeat. At that point, the Japanese proposed an armistice, which was quickly accepted by both the French and the Thais; hostilities were terminated by the end of the month.

Having closed the back door to China by moving forces into Tonkin, the Japanese next turned to exploiting Indochina's position as the gateway to Southeast Asia. For this purpose, the Japanese government addressed a series of new demands to the Vichy Government on 14 July 1941. The French, pressed by the Germans at home and finding no visible means of support elsewhere, came to terms with the Japanese more quickly than before. The agreements reached in late July permitted the Japanese to deploy unspecified numbers of troops into the country in addition to using eight airfields in south Indochina and the naval facilities at Saigon and Cam Ranh Bay. In short, Indochina became the springboard for the invasion of Thailand, Malaya, and Burma.

The United States' reaction to this development was the signing of an executive order on 26 July freezing all Japanese funds and assets in the United States. This was followed by notification to Japan that the Panama Canal would be closed for repairs. Further, Philippine military forces were mustered into service with the United States Army. Finally, on the first of August, the President of the United States issued an order prohibiting the shipment to Japan of a list of strategic materials, which included petroleum products suitable for use as aviation fuels. Thus, positions hardened and, although negotiations between the United States and Japan were continued, the course toward Pearl Harbor on 7 December had been set.

The war in the Pacific began with a series of wide-ranging surprise attacks. The attack against the Hawaiian Islands was the task of Vice Admiral Nagumo's Pearl Harbor Striking Force, which was based in home waters. Guam and Wake were the targets of Admiral Inouye's 4th Fleet, coming from Truk. Hong Kong was invaded by three divisions under

Lieutenant General Sakai Takashi, which had earlier moved opposite that Crown Colony. General Homma led his 14th Army to the Philippines, striking Luzon from Formosa and Mindanão from Palau. Finally, Indochina was the launching point for General Yamashita's 25th Army, aimed at Malaya and Singapore and for the Imperial Guards Division which advanced across Thailand to open the way into Burma for General Iida's 15th Army.

As a consequence of these events, the 30,000 European civilians in Indochina found themselves in the precarious position of living in the midst of a local population with strong nationalist tendencies and a Japanese military community that looked upon the area as its own. Moreover, the French in Indochina were isolated from the stream of events in Europe and Africa and were late to feel the stimulus of the French resistance movement.

For the Japanese, Indochina was a source of supplies and a well-situated base. Since these assets could be exploited with little difficulty, it served their purpose to allow the French to retain the outward trappings of authority. This, however, was unsatisfactory to the Free French who, from the time they had renewed their struggle against the Axis in Africa, entertained the hope of an early liberation of Indochina. These hopes began to take form in the fall of 1943 when a decision was made to organize an Expeditionary Corps for operations in the Far East. At the same time, French military personnel joined Force 136, an organization created by the British in India for covert and commando-type operations in Southeast Asia. In similar fashion, another French group had been established in Kunming in south China, initially to maintain contact with French elements in Indochina and, later, to provide the basis for an agent net extending along the northern Indochinese border areas.

Liaison between these two French groups in the Far East was complicated by the Allied Command arrangements which placed Indochina in the China theater. This, while technically under Generalissimo Chiang Kai-Chek, was an area of American strategic responsibility.

There was thus a wide difference in attitudes toward the French serving in India under Admiral Mountbatten's sympathetic South East Asia Command and those forming Mission 5 in Kunming where the Americans, reflecting President Roosevelt's anticolonial views and particularly his reluctance to see the French return to Indochina, were cool and reserved.

Despite all difficulties, a resistance in Indochina did develop and, as the tide of war in the Pacific turned against the Japanese, the French became increasingly defiant. This situation eventually became intolerable to the Japanese and on 9 March 1945 they struck against the French garrisons in that country. The French losses in these actions were heavy, but by May some 6000 troops, mostly Europeans, had fought their way out and were regrouped in south China.

The Japanese then turned to native political figures to establish the forms of new government. On 11 March, Bao Dai heir of the ancient ruling dynasty proclaimed the independence of the Empire of Annam, uniting Tonkin and Annam under the old name of Vietnam. This was followed on 13 March by the declaration of independence of the King of Cambodia; that of the King of Laos followed on 20 April. Admittedly, Cambodia and Laos enjoyed a considerable degree of freedom since there were few Japanese in those countries. However, there was little self rule in Vietnam, and the weakness of the Bao Dai regime was emphasized both by the unwillingness of many nationalists to support it and by the direct control of Cochinchina which the Japanese retained.

The lack of popular support for Bao Dai is readily explained by what had been happening to nationalist groups in Indochina. In the course of the preceding years, several of these groups — including the communists in 1940 — had attempted uprisings that had all been put down by the French. As a consequence, many of the revolutionaries involved had then made their way to south China where, in 1941, they began to consolidate under the leadership of Ho Chi Minh as the Vietnam Independence League. This association, called Viet Minh in abbreviated form, was too far to the left to enjoy the confidence of Generalissimo Chiang

Kai-Chek and in late 1942 a more docile coalition group, the Vietnam Revolutionary League, was formed under Chinese sponsorship. Ho Chi Minh had meanwhile been jailed by the Chinese as a French spy. He was released in 1943, and the work of organizing Viet Minh guerrilla forces and infiltrating them into north Vietnam was undertaken in earnest.

While the avowed purpose of the Viet Minh movements into north Vietnam was to fight the Japanese, it was evident that the real object was to drive out the French. This is affirmed by handbills, distributed in Moncay in March 1945, which stated that the Allies would destroy the Japanese and that it was for the Viet Minh to destroy the French, who were then in difficult straits. In any event, by May 1945 there were six provinces in Tonkin under Viet Minh control and, shortly before the collapse of Japan, the Viet Minh had organized a People's National Liberation Committee to set up a new regime.

The opportunity to implement these plans came during the month between mid-August when the Japanese capitulated and mid-September when the first British and Chinese occupation forces arrived in Saigon and Hanoi, respectively. On 25 August, Emperor Bao Dai signed the decree of abdication which transferred 'our authority to the Democratic Republican government'. This was followed on 2 September by the signing of a declaration of independence in Hanoi by Ho Chi Minh and his associates. The Republic of Vietnam thus created claimed authority over the whole of Vietnam to include Tonkin, Annam, and Cochinchina.

General Vo Nguyen Giap writes of these historic events in the following words:

> In August 1945, the capitulation of the Japanese forces before the Soviet Army and the Allied Forces put an end to the world war. The defeat of the German and Nippon fascists was the beginning of a great weakening of the capitalist system. After the great victory of the Soviet Union, many peoples' democracies saw the light of day. The socialist system was no longer confined within the frontiers of a single country. A new historic era was beginning in the world.

Above
Ships detachment from the French Navy aircraft carrier Bearn *lands in Indochina in 1945. These sailors were soon to see action with the naval brigade in clearing operations between Mytho and Saigon.* (ECPA)

Opposite above
A Saigon side street scene. Despite the eight years of the Indochina War, Saigon retained its pleasing aspect and moderate tempo of life. The Vietnam War, however, brought with it large population movements and economic imbalances that overwhelmed the city. This appears to be changing under the communist regime, but, when Saigon became Ho Chi Minh City it closed the door on its past forever.

Opposite
A French aircraft carrier in port at Saigon. At the time of the Indochina war, Saigon was accessible to ships drawing 9.3 meters (30 feet) and up to 180 meters (590 feet) in length.

In view of these changes, in Viet Nam, the Indochinese Communist Party and the Viet Minh called the whole Vietnamese nation to general insurrection. Everywhere, the people rose in a body. Demonstrations and displays of force followed each other uninterruptedly. In August, the Revolution broke out, neutralising the bewildered Nippon troops, overthrowing the pro-Japanese feudal authorities, and installing peoples' power in Hanoi and throughout the country, in the towns as well as in the countryside, in Bac Bo [North Vietnam], as well as in Nam Bo [South Vietnam]. In Hanoi, the capital, in [sic] September 2nd, the provisional government [sic] was formed around President Ho Chi Minh; it presented itself to the nation, proclaimed the independence of Viet Nam, and called on the nation to unite, to hold itself in readiness to defend the country and to oppose all attempts at imperialist aggression. The Democratic Republic of Viet Nam was born, the first peoples' democracy in Southeast Asia.

At the time of the Japanese capitulation, the French had some 700 military personnel in India available to accompany the Commonwealth forces ordered to occupation duties in Indochina below the 16th Parallel. An initial detachment of 150 French landed with the Ghurka Brigade at Tan Son Nhut airfield on 12 September 1945. The remainder were embarked on the French warship *Richelieu* and landed on 2 October with the other two Commonwealth brigades at Cap St Jacques (Vung Tau).

The situation in Saigon had been tense for some time and, when clashes broke out between the French and Vietnamese, the British commander, General Gracey, imposed martial law. He also freed and rearmed the French troops whom the Japanese had interned a few months before. On 23 September, the reinforced French were able to regain control of the public buildings in Saigon and resume administration of the city. Resistance on the part of the Vietnamese against the French nevertheless continued.

General Leclerc, who had represented France at the surrender ceremonies in

Tokyo, soon arrived in Saigon to assume command of French forces. On 15 October he flew to Cambodia, arrested the pro-Japanese premier, and cleared the way for a new government that on 7 January 1946 agreed to the return of French control over the country.

On 22 October, the initial element of the French Expeditionary Corps proper, a combat command from the 2nd Armored Division, began debarking in Saigon. This was followed in November by the 9th Colonial Infantry Division and in December by a brigade from Madagascar. As these additional forces landed, General Leclerc quickly formed them into flying columns which he used to extend French control over the whole of Indochina south of the 16th Parallel. He realized that this control was at best tenuous, since the nationalist Viet Minh forces quickly reformed once the French forces had passed on. Nevertheless, he was anxious to reintroduce the French presence throughout the south to pave the way — psychologically, if nothing more — for the far more difficult task awaiting him in the north.

The return of the French in the south was facilitated by the cooperation of the British and the lack of firm control by the newly independent Vietnamese government over competing nationalist elements. The situation in the north was, however, far different.

As soon as word of the Japanese surrender reached Kunming, Jean Sainteny, the head of the French Mission there, made every effort to rush to Hanoi. Yet, when he did arrive on 22 August, he found there was little he could do. The government of Ho Chi Minh was firmly established in power, and the Chinese were expected to arrive momentarily to exercise their occupation functions. The return of the French thus became conditional on two counts: first, there had to be an agreement whereby French troops would replace Chinese forces, and second, there had to be some form of accord with the Vietnamese government.

The advance elements of approximately 200,000 troops that the Chinese were to despatch to Indochina north of the 16th Parallel to receive the surrender of some 35,000 Japanese arrived in Hanoi on 15 September. There then began

a period of systematic looting by the Chinese which, according to French estimates, involved the transfer of goods to China valued at more than 250 million Indochinese piasters. At the same time, certain Vietnamese nationalist groups returned from exile — notably the Dong Minh Hoi party, which enjoyed the support of the Chinese military and had sufficient strength so that it could not be ignored by Ho Chi Minh.

The French undertook negotiations with the Chinese in Chungking and, at the cost of major concessions, reached an agreement on 28 February 1946 that per-

Right and Opposite
Below the latitude of Danang the highlands comprise an ancient crystalline massif with extensive lava flows, the latter particularly evident near Pleiku. These Southern Highlands are the home of the Mois, a Vietnamese term meaning savage or primitive. These simple mountain people are divided into numerous tribes and clans representing fragments of Austro-Asiatic and Malayo-Polynesian ethnic groups. This lack of homogeneity is reflected in a long history of inter-tribal conflict and indifferent respect for government authority whether French or Vietnamese. The Viet Minh were no more successful in controlling them. Ngo Dinh Diem recognized that, while the Mois were minorities, their allegiance would help keep the highlands quiet. He thus visited the main Moi population centers. At the right, he is seen being received by local notables, while opposite, is shown a Moi reception committee for Diem which included a gong band: rapid beating of the gongs causes a not unpleasant pulsating sound.

Opposite below
Lt General Samuel T. Williams, U.S. Army, Chief of the U.S. Military Assistance and Advisory Group, contemplates freshly cut haunch of barely cooked water buffalo and several jars of rice wine being offered by village officials to the Premier and his party.

Below
Moi reception group awaiting Premier Diem's arrival.

mitted them to move military forces into Indochina north of the 16th Parallel. In this the French were probably assisted indirectly by Chiang Kai-Chek's need of his troops for operations against Chinese communist forces in China. During this same period, there had been a series of conversations between the French and Ho Chi Minh in which it was evident there were compelling reasons for tolerance and compromise on both sides. Eventually, this led to a 'preliminary agreement', which was signed in Hanoi on 6 March 1946, whereby France recognized the Democratic Republic of Vietnam as a 'free state of the Indochinese Federation within the French Union', and the Vietnamese government declared itself '... ready to welcome in friendly fashion the French Army when, in conformance with international agreement, it would relieve the Chinese forces ...'.

The conclusion of the preliminary Franco-Vietnamese agreement of 6 March removed the last legal obstacle to the return of the French and, on the very day it was signed, the first of the 15,000 French and 10,000 Vietnamese troops that were to be allowed north of the 16th Parallel began landing in Haiphong. The French forces entered Hanoi on 18 March and soon after there were French garrisons in Tourane (Danang), Hue, and Lang Son. Additionally, the forces that had been regrouped in south China returned and occupied Phong Saly and

Sam Neua in Laos and the China border-area towns of Lai Chau and Moncay. In sum, in a little more than six months the French had reoccupied major strategic points throughout Indochina. Peace, however, had not been restored.

In April 1946, a Vietnamese delegation reached Paris to elaborate upon the preliminary agreement of 6 March concerning 'the future status of Indochina' and the 'diplomatic relations of Vietnam with foreign powers'. These were issues that had been left pending despite their major importance to Vietnamese sovereignty. During the prolonged negotiations that ensued, the divergence of views between the French and Vietnamese and the firmness of their positions made any satisfactory compromise impossible. However, when the rest of the Vietnamese delegation returned to Haiphong on 3 October empty handed, Ho Chi Minh, who had participated in many of the discussions during the previous months, remained in France to make a final effort to salvage something from this unhappy and inconclusive period. The result of this final gesture was a 'modus vivendi', signed on 14 September 1946, which prescribed interim measures intended to harmonize relations between the French and Vietnamese pending the resumption of negotiations in January 1947.

The situation in Vietnam meanwhile had been deteriorating, and there was little hope that policies of moderation and

conciliation could continue to be entertained. During the four months that Ho Chi Minh had been away from Vietnam, his deputy, Vo Nguyen Giap, had consolidated the power of the Viet Minh in the north and largely destroyed the prospects for any adjustment of the basic differences with the French. Indeed there was even a period when Ho Chi Minh was labeled a traitor to the cause of Vietnamese independence because of his dealings with the French. By the time that Ho Chi Minh returned to Vietnam aboard a French warship on 21 October, the two final acts that were to lead to open warfare were only a few weeks away.

The first of these occurred in November when the French Navy seized a junk presumed to be loaded with contraband. This touched off the question of control of customs, which was already a sensitive issue between the French and Vietnamese. In the violence that quickly followed, the French undertook operations to clear the city of Haiphong and caused heavy casualties among the civilian population. The second act was a series of violent surprise attacks launched by Viet Minh forces against the French in Hanoi during the evening of 19 December. Open fighting then broke out throughout much of Indochina. Despite later attempts at negotiations, the rupture between the French and Vietnamese was complete. The Indochina War had begun.

PART 2
THE INDO-CHINA
WAR

4

The French Experience

The southern Chinese, kin to the Vietnamese, were known well before the Christian era as a people who used boats and oars rather than carts and horses to travel to far places. Despite this heritage and the ever present influence of deltaic and coastal environments, the communist Viet Minh confined themselves in this century to developing a highly effective land army. Only the French and the Vietnamese National Army they created took to the coastal and inland waters of Indochina for military purposes.

When the Indochina War officially began on 19 December 1946, the 30,000 man French Expeditionary Corps had suffered cruel losses in dead and wounded over the preceding eighteen months. Many of these casualties had been sustained in the south where the widespread terrorism that had prevailed since September 1945 had intensified once France had decided to keep Cochinchina separate from Vietnam. This had been formalized on 1 June 1946 with the establishment of the French supported Republic of Cochinchina.

On the outbreak of general hostilities at the end of 1946, General Giap commanded some 60,000 communist troops, organized into thirty-five regiments of infantry and three of artillery; 12,000 of these were in Cochinchina. The French had the 3rd Colonial Infantry Division to cover this same region. This was completely inadequate even though several provinces were controlled by independent sect forces such as the Cao Dai and Hoa Hao. In Annam, the French had two infantry battalions while, in Tonkin, 13,000 French faced over 30,000 Viet Minh.

Despite their numerical inferiority, the French were far better equipped than the communist formations and were able to meet all attacks. Nonetheless, they quickly concluded that, while immediate rein-

forcement of the Expeditionary Corps was necessary, the conflict could only be resolved by political means. This realization was accompanied by the idea of creating a new national government to oppose that of Ho Chi Minh.

In seeking to demonstrate their return over as great an area as possible, the French had deployed their forces throughout Indochina. The positive psychological impact of this dispersal quickly vanished when the war broke out. The problem for the French then became that

of consolidating their scattered units while retaining control over critical areas and key positions and making available mobile reserves to carry the war to the enemy. The contradiction in requirements for area control as opposed to those for mobile warfare were to plague the French throughout the eight years of the Indochina War.

During the first month of the war, the French reopened the road link between Hanoi and Haiphong, strengthened their hold over towns near the China border,

The operational environment. *The French had to cope with three major factors in their operational environment: the first was the physical demands of the country; the second, the limit on resources both as to quantity and type; the third, the heterogeneous composition of the French Union Forces. To overcome these factors required exceptional ingenuity, innovation, tolerance and understanding. The nature of the last quality may be appreciated by the fact that a Vietnamese parachutist weighed one third less than a European. Thus, when using parachutes intended for Europeans, a Vietnamese was much more likely to be affected by even light surface winds. Another area where understanding was needed was in the matter of diet, and in particular when related to religious feast days. Thus, live sheep were air lifted from Morocco and delivered to Moroccan units for their use in religious ceremonials.*

Above right
A French patrol uses native boats to move on shallow narrow waterways near Mytho in Cochinchina in 1950. (ECPA)

Right
A STCAN/FOM patrol boat of Dinassaut 12 protects Vietnamese troops engaged in building a bamboo bridge over the Rach Binh to facilitate the crossing of the 1st Moroccan Infantry Battalion; Tonkin, 16 May 1951. (ECPA)

Opposite
Troops of the 3rd Battalion, 5th Foreign Legion Regiment, prepare to cross the Black River on 14 November 1951 during the Hoa Binh offensive. Note use of pontoon bridge sections and that the monitor has a tank turret mounted forward. The usual armament of the monitor was the 40 mm cannon. However, some turrets taken off light Italian tanks captured in World War II were also used. (ECPA)

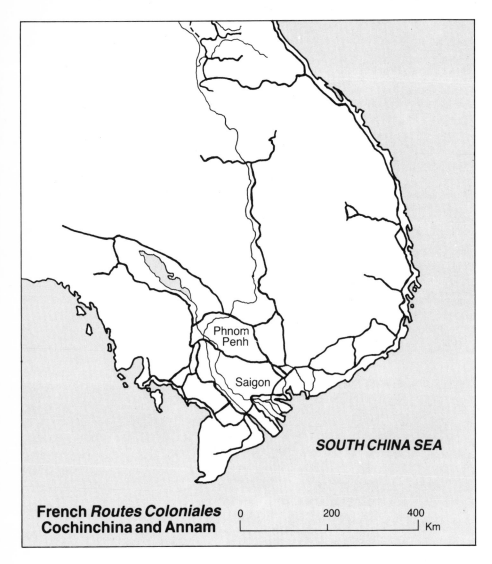

**French *Routes Coloniales*
Cochinchina and Annam**

SOUTH CHINA SEA

Phnom
Penh

Saigon

0   200   400
|_____|_____| Km

On the eve of World War II when comparative statistics were available, the roadnet of Tonkin, Annam and Cochinchina was recorded as 6800, 7000 and 7700 kilometers respectively, of which 2400 kilometers of 'routes coloniales' are shown on the map. The navigable waterways of the same period for the same order of regions are given as 3300, 3000 and 3900 kilometers. The development of the roadnet was largely due to the French who wished to link the major administrative divisions of Indochina. The waterways were the principal means of transportation before the French occupation and remained of major economic importance because they served to meet local transportation requirements.

and reinforced their garrison at Nam Dinh some 80 kilometers below Hanoi on the Red River. This last operation involved a two hundred man parachute drop south of the city coordinated with the assault landing of a reinforced Foreign Legion rifle company moving by river; the whole conducted under air cover. This type of operation was charac-

teristic of many that were to follow, the principal variations being in the size of the forces engaged and whether the ground elements moved by road or river, or by both.

While operations to consolidate forces were proceeding in the northern delta, a succession of sharp engagements were fought in Annam to clear Tourane (Danang), raise the prolonged siege of Hue, and gain control of the 100 kilometer coastline in between. This latter effort, later extended over a 300 kilometer coastal zone, involved a series of amphibious envelopments linking up with forces moving overland. In one such operation a rifle company of the 23rd Colonial Infantry Regiment stopped by an enemy position on the Truoi River slipped 3 kilometers upriver, crossed the river by swimming, and successfully attacked the position from the rear.

During this first month of the war there was little change in Cochinchina because both sides lacked the resources for other than sporadic and inconclusive incidents. In France, during this period, the government concluded that the conflict in Indochina no longer consisted simply of acts of terrorism. Emile Bollaert was designated High Commissioner and sent to Saigon with instruction to seek negotiations, while using the military to maintain order and ensure the garrisons' security and lines of communications.

Ho Chi Minh declared himself willing to negotiate if the French first recognized the independence and unity of Vietnam (i.e. with Cochinchina included). The French in turn asked Ho to surrender his weapons, which he refused to do. While these abortive maneuvers were taking place during March 1947, the French were reinforcing their Expeditionary Corps. By the first of April it had reached 100,000 men. Of its sixty-nine infantry battalions twenty-three were then assigned to Cochinchina.

Despite the generous share of the Expeditionary Corps in the south, the French still lacked the equipment to operate on the waterways. Moreover, under orders of the civil authority, the French military were to establish some 500 posts. Further, French forces were to concentrate in the west where the population and rice growing areas were most numerous. The military command had little left with which to move into the center of the delta, where major enemy forces were operating. There was thus a conflict between the civil attitude toward the peace keeping posture the military were to adopt and the military, who were most concerned with the classic mission of finding and destroying the enemy.

To mitigate the difficulty, the French reached agreements with two religious sects that maintained independent militias. The well organized Cao Dai were invited to keep the peace in their province of Tay Ninh with their 4500 man army; a similar arrangement was reached with the Hoa Hao, whose army numbered only 2500.

While the French High Commissioner was waging his peace offensive in the south, General Valluy in the north had concluded that the Viet Minh represented a centralized organization dependent on broadly-based popular support. He proposed to destroy this relationship by launching a major offensive against the northern mountain stronghold where Ho Chi Minh and his government had taken refuge after moving out of the Tonkin delta area.

The French by then had further increased the strength of the Expeditionary Corps to 115,000 men. Valluy estimated his autumn offensive would require 50,000 men. Notwithstanding the new reinforcements, Valluy was limited to 32,000 men, of which only 12,000 could be used for mobile operations. Valluy's plan had to be scaled down, but the effort launched on 20 September was still impressive. In ten days the French had 10,000 men positioned along a 400 kilometer periphery to control the principal access routes of the communist enclave. That operation had required a navy river flotilla to move a 2300 man force up the Red River and a 2200 man force up the Clear River, while a motor transport battalion moved an equivalent force by road. The net was to be closed by a parachute battalion dropped near where Ho had been reported.

The plan succeeded in its outline. But, as was to happen again and again, the French had too few forces to close the trap effectively. The Viet Minh were able to work their way out through the gaps in the French dispositions and in numerous instances they were able to strike at the dispersed French units, notably the force moving on the Clear River. As a result, the members of the Viet Minh government escaped and some 16,000 communist troops made their way down country to Thai Nguyen where they regrouped. From there, they soon began to threaten the communications of the French units still in the uplands. Nonetheless, in something over a month of maneuvering and fighting, the French had disrupted the enemy government and captured one of its ministers. They had also seized and destroyed many small arms factories and captured sizeable stocks of supplies and communications equipment. These last were particularly serious since the Viet Minh were hard pressed to obtain the resources for their military operations.

No sooner were major communist

INDOCHINA
French Administrative Divisions and the Mekong and Red River Deltas
Dates refer to year of French occupation

forces identified in the Thai Nguyen area than the French launched an 8000 man force against them. Again the operation involved two main forces moving by river. Other light forces were to move overland and a parachute drop was planned near Thai Nguyen itself once the ground units were in position. The weather, however, delayed the air operation and by the time it could be launched the Viet Minh had safely withdrawn.

As 1947 ended, the French had strengthened their hold on most of the population centers and key areas of the country. They had not, however, been able to destroy the Viet Minh Army nor even bring it to battle. Such combat as had occurred had been costly (over 5000 dead and nearly 10,000 wounded) but none had been conclusive. Still, the Viet Minh had been badly battered and the year end balance favoured the French.

This might have appeared as the proper time to settle matters by negotiating with the Ho government. But, on the contrary, the French decided to cease

39

efforts to communicate with that government and seek instead an arrangement with Bao Dai, the hereditary Emperor of Vietnam. Bao Dai, like Ho Chi Minh, wanted an independent Vietnam to include Cochinchina. Both leaders also were concerned with what the French meant by independence within the French Union. Bao Dai was therefore cautious and noncommital in his dealings with the French. Moreover, it was evident that the National Vietnamese Party which represented all non Viet Minh elements had a large membership but little real cohesiveness. It was a poor foundation upon which to expect Bao Dai to build a national government. Still, optimism prevailed and the French began to reduce their Expeditionary Corps.

The Ho government had been unable to establish itself firmly in Cochinchina before the French returned. To strengthen its position the Viet Minh intensified its guerrilla activity in this area, even as their main battle force was evading the French in Tonkin. The general insecurity in Cochinchina that resulted, coupled with the opening moves to form a government under Bao Dai, caused the French to shift their principal effort to the south. Thus, when operations in the Thai Nguyen area ceased, the French moved four battalions south to begin a campaign of pacification, counter guerrilla, and search and destroy operations.

The objective of the French in Cochinchina was to isolate the Viet Minh from the people and develop a support base for the Bao Dai government.

Despite the shift of forces from the north and the assignment of only six battalions to control Annam, the forces of the Expeditionary Corps available in the south remained too few to carry on all the tasks required. Some economies were made possible, however, by increasing the support for the sect forces. The Cao Dai were raised to a strength of 7300 men and some of the units were assigned pacification tasks outside their home province of Tay Ninh. The forces of the less cohesive Hoa Hao were not increased significantly but they were reorganized and assigned advisors to improve their effectiveness. The Catholic minorities were also encouraged to organize the defense of their communities and a Chris-

tian Mobile Defense Force of 2500 men was created.

These measures enabled the French to assemble sufficient mobile forces to seek out and destroy the communist power center in the Plain of Reeds, which straddles the border between Vietnam and Cambodia and extends deep into the former. Operation 'Vega', begun on 14 February 1948, committed eleven battalions of infantry, supported by four naval assault divisions and two companies of 'crabs'. These last were light, tracked vehicles (US designation M29 Weasel) particularly well suited to operations in swamp areas. The vast encirclement maneuver went as planned, but after four days there were no Viet Minh in the net. Only one pocket of communist resistance had been encountered and this had been quickly destroyed by a unit of 'crabs'. While no significant Viet Minh forces had been found, 'Vega' nonetheless enabled the French to destroy stocks of equipment and supplies. The operation also convinced the French that such efforts were unprofitable. They thenceforth engaged principally in local actions to support the system of posts and their lines of communications as part of their campaign of pacification in Cochinchina.

A French outpost looking toward China on high ground near the coast.

It was in this same mid-1948 period that the Viet Minh attacked the Binh Xuyen in the Rung Sat area near Saigon. As a result, this predatory band of river pirates decided to offer their independent forces to the French.

In the north, meanwhile, Ho Chi Minh had decentralized the politico-military structure of his government to reduce its vulnerability to any future French offensive. Ho also turned to extensive guerrilla activity to harass the French in their northern border positions. These were recognized by both the French and Viet Minh to be of growing importance in the light of Chinese communist thrusts southward. The French military command, indeed, anticipated that Chinese communists would reach the border of Vietnam in 1949 and wanted to undertake an operation to clear and consolidate their hold on the border area before that could happen.

The political scene in France was confused and Indochina far away. Under these circumstances no decisions were forthcoming other than to continue efforts to rally the population in support of a Bao Dai government. Further complications arose because of differences among the generals over whether to concentrate the military effort in Tonkin in the highlands or in the Red River delta, where there was a widespread resurgence

40

A temporary dinassaut base in the Plain of Reeds. Note the flat terrain making distant observation difficult and complicating the defense problem. (ECPA)

of Viet Minh guerrilla activity. In any event, pending the arrival of reinforcements it was only possible for the French to engage in preliminary operations to reopen communications between the delta and up-country garrisons.

An initial air and naval strike was launched near Thanh Hoa on the coast, in the southern part of the Red River delta at the end of October. This was followed on 7 November by Operation 'Ondine' in the western part of the delta and the foothills area. On that date, a parachute battalion was dropped on Vietri and two battalions of infantry embarked in a naval assault division moved up the Red River to seize Son Tay and effect a link up. On 19 November yet another force was moved up the Black River toward Hoa Binh in parallel with a battalion marching by road. Then, in December, the French seized Phu Ly on the

southern edge of the delta. The first phase of the campaign had ended and the French position had substantially improved.

The reinforcements required to extend operations in the highlands were slow in arriving. At this same time, the High Commissioner in Saigon opposed further action in Tonkin and Annam and directed that the military effort be again concentrated in Cochinchina at the beginning of 1949. Even so, the French did not have the resources to destroy major Viet Minh units. They thus returned to their pursuit of local engagements in support of a system of posts intended to maintain control of land and water communications.

In the political arena, the French government agreed on 23 April 1949 to include Cochinchina in an independent Vietnam. This removed the last obstacle

to the return of Bao Dai and he landed in Dalat five days later.

Then, as the French were actively engaged in pacification operations in the south, the number of incidents in the highlands of Tonkin began to multiply. Chiang Kai-Chek had resigned in January and the presence of Chinese communist forces on the Vietnam border encouraged Viet Minh ambitions. This same presence, and particularly the Chinese raid on the Vietnamese coastal town of Moncay, caused the French to add thirteen more battalions to the reinforcements being sent to Indochina. The French, however, remained undecided on the best course of action to follow.

To address the matter, the French gov-

41

ernment despatched General Revers to Indochina on 13 May 1949. On 29 June, the General submitted a critical report which proposed the creation of a Vietnamese National Army to carry on pacification and the consolidation of the responsibilities of the High Commissioner and Commander in Chief of French Union Forces, Indochina in one man. General Revers also stressed the vital importance of denying the Viet Minh support from the Chinese communists. He urged that the French center their military effort in Tonkin to accomplish that objective. He further noted that such action would create a favourable climate in which to request military assistance from the United States, with whom the North Atlantic Treaty had just been signed.

General Revers' military recommendations were approved and plans were made to clear a triangle in the north roughly bounded by the Red River, the coast, and a section of the Chinese border. The plan also envisaged that the French would withdraw their forces from the more remote mountainous positions, notably Cao Bang, which could not be properly supported.

In the south, earlier French operations in the Plain of Reeds had caused the Viet Minh to move their major installations to Camau on the southernmost tip of Cochinchina. Still, the Plain of Reeds remained useful to the communists as a transit area. When in June 1949 the French identified four Viet Minh battalions in the Plain they immediately launched a 4000 man force to attack them. This time the French force included two amphibious companies made up of infantry embarked in World War II tracked landing vehicles (LVT). This maneuver element enabled the French to fix the communist force and in the fight that ensued the Viet Minh lost 500 dead and 130 prisoners.

This success came as Bao Dai arrived in Saigon where he undertook to form a government, which was established on 12 July 1949. Following formation of the new government, Bao Dai made trips to Hue and Hanoi. This progress in the domain of political affairs was welcome but not conclusive. Bao Dai was far from being a rallying point for the non communist Vietnamese. And the French,

who appeared unable to devise and pursue a coherent policy in Indochina, had failed to destroy the Viet Minh, who now had the priceless advantage of sympathetic Chinese nearby.

In July of that year, the French began a succession of operations in the Tonkin delta to extend their control over the approaches to the highlands. Coincident with these, the French abandoned their isolated frontier posts and brought their forces into Cao Bang and Dong Khe which, in a reversal of General Revers' recommendation, were now to be held. Lastly, the French occupied the Catholic provinces along the southern coast of the Tonkin delta where they soon gained the adherence of the local population.

Even as the French were engaged in this widespread military and political activity they were confronted with thousands of Chinese nationalist troops and civilians fleeing before the communist armies. Mao Tse Tung had announced the establishment of the Chinese People's Republic in October 1949 and warned off anyone offering assistance to the nationalists. The French, understandably apprehensive over this threat, nonetheless agreed to receive 34,300 nationalist troops. These were initially interned at Campha on the north Vietnam coast, then transferred to the island of Phu Quoc off southern Vietnam, and finally sent to Taiwan in 1953.

The new government in Peiping was quickly recognized by all communist countries in November 1949, but, interestingly, Ho Chi Minh took two months before following suit. However, by January 1950 both Ho and Mao had acknowledged each others' governments and Russia had declared itself ready to enter into diplomatic relations with the Democratic Republic of Vietnam.

The French, meanwhile, had agreed to transfer the administrative responsibilities of government to Bao Dai and the new Vietnamese flag had been raised over Saigon. Recognition of the Bao Dai government by the United States and Great Britain was extended on 7 February 1950; other western democracies followed shortly thereafter. During the same month the Sino-Soviet alliance came into being and Ho declared general mobilization.

Then, in April, the Chinese began to provide military assistance to the Viet Minh. At the same time, the Americans agreed to help the Associated States of Indochina. The French, however, preferred such aid to flow through French channels. It was not until 30 June 1950 that the issue was resolved and the first delivery of seven C-47 aircraft reached the French Expeditionary Corps. The Indochina War had clearly been internationalized.

Concurrent with these far reaching developments, Viet Minh forces had engaged numerous well-coordinated offensive actions in the highlands of Tonkin and the upper Red River basin. They had also undertaken a war of movement in Annam and Cochinchina that extended from December 1949 to April 1950. Fifteen Viet Minh battalions had been committed in a succession of actions in Cochinchina alone, where they displayed an aggressiveness and tenacity not previously witnessed. In one such engagement on 26 March 3000 communists left 400 dead before withdrawing in the face of crushing firepower. The combat qualities of the Viet Minh were of high order but again the superior fire power and the mobility of the French proved decisive.

The communist campaign in Cochinchina was inconclusive. It did, however, provide their forces in Tonkin the time to prepare themselves for operations that were to cause the French exceptional losses later that year. In Cochinchina, meanwhile, the French strategy of holding the Mekong to isolate the communist stronghold in Camau from the piedmont and central highlands had proven effective and the high losses suffered by the Viet Minh were facilitating the French task of pacification.

The French Expeditionary Corps had reached the strength of 150,000 in early 1950, but the French government was hard pressed to maintain such a force in the light of its other commitments, notably those deriving from its membership in NATO. Thus, the forces in Indochina were urged to consolidate their positions and scale down their operations. Particular attention was also to be given to the nurturing of the Vietnamese army, which was intended to relieve the French of

pacification responsibilities in favor of mobile operations.

As events unfolded in Cochinchina, most often in favor of the French, the French were able to assemble twenty infantry battalions, which they used during the first six months of 1950 to clear and consolidate their hold over the Tonkin delta. The Viet Minh riposted with widespread attacks that caused painful losses but otherwise only demonstrated the improved combat effectiveness resulting from the arrival of Chinese-supplied weaponry.

In the summer of 1950, the French could gain considerable satisfaction from their control over key areas of Indochina and the growing strength of the Bao Dai government and its embryo national army. Equally reassuring was the steady arrival of American military equipment. Then, on 25 June, North Korea invaded South Korea and the Indochina War, which had already become international-ized, became part of a greater anti communist struggle.

The military situation in Indochina was clearly stabilized, but this could not endure for the base upon which this stability rested was fragile. In France, yet another government, the twelfth since 1945, had come to power. In France, too, the parliament had made the High Council of the French Union the directing body of a federation rather than a confederation. This was not reassuring to the representatives of the Associated States of Indochina who were to meet at Pau, in southwest France, at the end of June to define the political status of the member states within the French Union. The Americans, who had agreed reluctantly to channel aid to Indochina through the French, were also encouraging the broadest possible interpretation of independence for the Associated States.

Most disturbing as an immediate and direct concern was the failure of the French to destroy the Viet Minh before Chinese communist assistance became available to them. Already in the May-to-September period 20,000 Viet Minh had received training in China and increasing stores of weapons and ammunitions were flowing south. Thus, while the Viet Minh military was being greatly strenghtened, the French were tying down ever larger numbers of their troops in the pacification mission that had been given the highest priority. Time favored the communists. This was painfully evident in the highlands where the French, after vacillating for a year over the question of withdrawing their exposed garrisons, were now hard pressed to keep them supplied.

Finally, in September, the French decided to evacuate Cao Bang. Since the forces involved included native units with families it was impossible to make the move by air; the withdrawal, which was to start 1 October, would have to be made by difficult overland routes exposed to enemy attack. On 16 September, the Viet Minh took Dong Khe some 45 kilometers below Cao Bang on the withdrawal route. The French then decided to retake Dong Khe with the force that was to support the withdrawal, before beginning to move the garrison out of Cao Bang. This extended the duration of the withdrawal, originally planned as a swift secret maneuver, with the result that the Viet Minh were able to destroy the French forces while still separated. The action was a catastrophe costing the French 4800 men killed and missing. This disaster was made even worse by the hasty evacuation of Lang Son, a town well below Dong Khe where the French abandoned 1300 tons of ammunition, fuel and other supplies.

The repercussions of this French setback were far reaching. A leading French political figure proclaimed the French policy in Indochina unrealistic in that it rested on a military effort without the resources necessary to force a decision and a political effort incapable of gaining popular support. Others saw Indochina as a no-win situation since Vietnam would gain its independence either under Bao Dai if the National Army and the French were to win or under Ho Chi Minh if the Viet Minh prevailed. In the event, the French again decided to strengthen the Expeditionary Corps which, in September, already totalled 166,000. They also agreed to raise the Vietnamese National Army to a strength of 115,000 men in 1951. Finally, General de Lattre de Tassigny was invited to take on the dual roles of High Commissioner and Commander-in-Chief of French Union Forces in Indochina.

The general landed in Saigon on 17 December 1950. From there he launched a whirlwind of personal visits to restore the shaken confidence of the French military command. He announced the war was one of liberation, that there would be no more retreat, and that the main effort would henceforth be in the north. Even as these declarations were being made, the Viet Minh launched strong attacks along the Chinese border toward the sea and down the valley of the Red River. The reaction of de Lattre was immediate and violent. He counter-attacked the force heading for the coast, making use of all available naval support and smashed the larger group moving down the Red River. In the latter action the communists lost 1500 dead and 480 prisoners, while the French casualties in killed, missing and wounded totalled 700.

The improved offensive capabilities of the Viet Minh formations decided General de Lattre to build a system of strong points to cover the northern delta. Eventually, some 900 such positions, able to withstand the strongest anticipated assault, were built. The effectiveness of the system rested only in part on the strong points; mobile forces were needed to complement the fixed defenses. To meet this need, the call went out to France for more troops. Additionally, seven battalions of infantry were sent to Tonkin from Cochinchina as more and more of the pacification responsibility in the south passed to Vietnamese units.

In March 1951 the Viet Minh embarked on an offensive operation against Dong Trieu, along the northern border of the delta between Hanoi and the coast, which was intended to lure the French into a vast ambush. The French responded with massive air strikes and the commitment of a naval assault division to reinforce the beleagured garrison. The French counter-attacks succeeded and by April, after bitter fighting, the Viet Minh withdrew. The French then launched two large-scale operations in succession, 'Meduse' and 'Reptile', to clear threatened areas of the delta. These proved inconclusive.

General de Lattre intended from the first to enlist the support of Bao Dai in a public relations type campaign to demonstrate Franco-Vietnamese solidarity and the mutuality of objectives. Bao Dai had proven lukewarm to these overtures and the population indifferent. Nonetheless, de Lattre persisted and among the measures taken he ordered each battalion of the Expeditionary Corps to sponsor the organization of a Vietnamese battalion. He also established the training facilities and schools needed to support the rapidly growing Vietnamese National Army. Then, at the Singapore Conference in mid-May, he made much of the need for cooperation among the British, French and Americans in the defence of Southeast Asia.

Shortly thereafter, at the end of May, the Viet Minh, rested and refitted after their abortive spring offensive, began new moves in the southern part of the Tonkin delta below Hanoi. The enemy aim was to advance across the Day River and smash the French forces concentrated in the area. The key to the French position was the river town of Ninh Binh to the south of the Day River. But, the battle which thwarted the communist advance occurred in the nearby town of Yen Cu Ha, which was on a tributary of the Day.

In each critical aspect of this campaign, the embattled inland navy of the French played a significant role. On the night of 28/29 May 1951, when the communists first crossed the Day at many points, a dinassaut quickly landed its marines in besieged Ninh Binh and stood by to give fire support. On the following morning all but 19 of the original 80 marines landed had been killed, and bazooka and recoilless cannon fire from the river banks had severely damaged some of the dinassaut craft. But the key position of Ninh Binh still remained in French hands. The focus of action then shifted to neighboring Yen Cu Ha. Here again a dinassaut was at the center of the battle and the flagship of the unit, an LSSL, was credited with saving this key position with its concentrated gunfire.

The dinassauts were naval assault divisions organized for assault landings, the patrol of waterways and the convoy of supplies. A number of these tasks complemented those of army units but dinassauts were used where combat power had priority importance, as in this campaign.

Inland seapower performed perhaps its most important mission in the campaign by wreaking havoc with the communist supply line across the Day River north of Ninh Binh. This line composed of small junks and sampans was attacked by the river forces which, together with French aircraft cut it to ribbons. By 18

Patrol of the 8th Company, 2nd Battalion, 43rd Colonial Infantry Regiment crosses the Rach Vien Si Muoi in Cochinchina on 1 June 1951. (ECPA)

June, the communist effort to capture the key posts of Ninh Binh and Yen Cu Ha had been repulsed. They had suffered heavy casualties and worst of all they were unable to maintain the forces they had succeeded in placing across the Day River because of the determined attacks by French river craft. The Viet Minh had no alternative but to retreat and thereby abandon a costly offensive. In just over two weeks of heavy fighting the Viet Minh had lost 1159 dead, 154 prisoners and an estimated 287 wounded. The French had lost 107 killed, among them young Lieutenant de Lattre, the general's own son.

The favorable balance of losses was encouraging to the French, but even with de Lattre's determined efforts, popular Vietnamese support for the anti communist war remained weak. To aggravate the situation, 1200 Cao Dai troops, resentful of French authority, took to the hills in July. At that same time General de Lattre returned to France for medical treatment. In September he undertook a long and successful trip to the United States, with short stopovers on his return in London and Rome, whereby he gained much public support for the French war effort. In October 1951 he was back in Vietnam, where the Viet Minh had once again thrust at French positions in the Tonkin delta.

General de Lattre reviewed the alternatives available to him and concluded he would strike beyond the delta to seize Hoa Binh. The town was an important communication center on the Black River some 60 kilometers west of Hanoi. In making this decision, and thus departing from his policy of limiting his operations to the delta proper, de Lattre hoped to encourage the French to allocate more funds to the war effort. He also believed this would influence the Americans to increase their military aid. Following a preparatory operation to position forces, de Lattre launched operation 'Lotus' on 14 November utilizing sixteen battalions of infantry and one naval assault division with strong artillery, armor and air support. In forty-eight hours the French had engaged 15,000 troops. Then, as de Lattre had planned, he was able to proclaim to the press that the operation had resulted in a great victory. Shortly thereafter General de Lattre returned to France where on 11 January 1952 he died. He had been suffering from cancer.

Whatever other value the French occupation of Hoa Binh may have had, it did disrupt Viet Minh plans to infiltrate large forces into the northern delta. The French had organized the defense of Hoa Binh around five infantry battalions. Another five battalions covered the approach along the Black River, while four battalions with armor covered the main land access road. The Viet Minh found this French intrusion intolerable and in December 1951 they repeatedly attacked the French forces. After bitter fighting they were able to deny the French the use of the river. The other French positions held but losses on both sides were becoming serious. Finally, in January 1952, after taking 800 casualties, over half in dead and missing, the French withdrew from their positions along the Black River. The Viet Minh had lost 1100 dead in these operations.

While these violent clashes were taking place in the Hoa Binh area, the Viet Minh were infiltrating large forces past the defending strong points into the delta proper. The delta area, a triangle roughly 150 kilometers on the side was the home of nine million people packed into 4000 villages. The French controlled the larger towns and their connecting roads, and supported the whole with a system of strong points and posts. The structure, however, was porous and as Viet Minh activity in the delta intensified, the

45

French decided on 5 February 1952 to withdraw from Hoa Binh.

The French had, in fact, already prepared to do so by reopening the land route linking Hoa Binh to the delta and causing debilitating losses to the three Viet Minh divisions in the area. Then from 14 to 20 February the French engaged in deception operations to convince the Viet Minh the French were consolidating their defenses of the land approach to Hoa Binh and the town itself. The real purpose was to enable the French to hold a crossing site over the Black River, a critical requirement for the evacuation. With all in order, operation 'Arc-en-Ciel' was launched at nightfall on 22 February 1952. All of its five phases, meticulously planned, were executed in text book fashion and the withdrawal was, deservedly, claimed to be a remarkable success.

During 1951 general mobilization and intensified French training support had enabled the Vietnamese National Army to reach a strength of 125,000, of which 54,000 were regular troops. The problem had not been the recruiting of personnel but rather the availability of equipment and cadres. Most critical was the shortage of officers, particularly in the senior ranks. Thus, by the end of the year only twenty of the thirty-five infantry battalions were commanded by Vietnamese. Still, these difficulties notwithstanding, the Vietnamese units performed well in combat and desertions proved far fewer than the French had anticipated.

This effort was paralleled on the communist side by measures that greatly enhanced Viet Minh capabilities. Reference has already been made to Chinese training and equipment support. This last was facilitated by the opening of a rail line from China to Lang Son in 1951, which enabled the Viet Minh to receive 4000 tons of supplies and equipment in the final four months of that year. The output over this rail line reached 15,000 tons in 1952.

Following the withdrawal from Hoa Binh, which cost the French less than one fifth the casualties taken in the Cao Bang evacuation, the French turned to the clearing of the Tonkin delta proper. A succession of mobile operations ensued. These, making much use of brown water navy units and amphibious vehicle formations, disrupted communist activities but seldom succeeded in inflicting heavy losses simply because the Viet Minh could always find their way out through gaps in the French dispositions.

The general pattern of operations was repeated in the Mekong delta where, in addition to fighting communists, the French had to struggle ceaselessly to retain the uncertain loyalty of the sect forces who continued unwillingly to be integrated into the National Army. Aggravating also to the French was the Plain of Reeds, whose control they could never ensure. Despite repeated French operations into the area, the communists continued to use it as a haven and transit route.

The situation in Annam was similar to that in Tonkin where the French conducted large scale ground, sea, and air operations. A number of these were along the 'street without joy', north of Hue. Another was the amphibious Operation 'Toulouse' launched against Qui Nhon, a coastal town in southern Annam in an area strongly held by the Viet Minh.

The Viet Minh appeared to be engaging the French in a war of attrition in 1952. They were in fact inflicting casualties particularly among junior officers at a rate the French found difficult to replace. Thus, although the Expeditionary Corps reached a peak strength of 189,000 that year, its quality was lessening. This was due in large measure to losses from combat and to the drain of officers and non commissioned officers represented by the advisory effort being made in support of the National Army.

Among the many operations carried out during the winter campaign of 1952–53 that of Na San was to establish a precedent leading to the final drama of the war. The French had noted that the communists took disproportionally high losses in attacking strongly defended positions. At the same time the French were finding that commando operations deep in Viet Minh country conducted by French led native units were proving surprisingly effective. Thus the idea was born of establishing an air supplied base in the uplands to improve further the capabilities of these native commando forces; Na San was selected for this purpose. When Na San was probed by the Viet Minh in October 1952, the French decided to reinforce and hold it.

Ten battalions of infantry with supporting units totalling 12,000 men were dug in at Na San. The force, entirely dependent on air supply from Hanoi some 200 kilometers away, required fifty supply flights per day. This, in October, ensured the delivery of 3000 tons of supplies. Thus, when General Giap mounted a determined attack on 30 November, Na San held and inflicted heavy losses on the Viet Minh. By 3 December, Giap had had enough and withdrew what remained of his battered units into Laos.

The winter campaign elsewhere extended into 1953 with operations repeating the pattern of those in the latter part of 1952. The French continued in their efforts to sanitize the populated areas (the northern and southern deltas and coastal enclaves between) to clear the way for pacification efforts by indigenous forces. The communists continued to terrorize and subvert the masses to counter the pacification. They also harassed French forces engaged in periodic sweeps of the lowlands and sought from time to time to attract French mobile units into the highlands. The Viet Minh offensive in Laos in April 1953 was one of the more ambitious of these operations. It proved to be of particular concern to the French for it revealed a substantial increase in Viet Minh strength.

The intensity and scale of operations of the French in this period were impressive. But, while each individual action generally favored the French, the collective result remained discouraging. Further, as the Vietnamese National Army assumed an ever greater share of the burden, it demanded less interference from the French. These factors all fueled a growing body of opinion in France that called for an end to the war. The death of Stalin in June and the armistice in Korea in July gave further impetus to the peace initiative.

It was in this climate of frustration and uncertainty that General Navarre arrived in Saigon as the new Commander-in-Chief on 8 May 1953. The general, a cavalry officer with no prior experience in Indochina, confronted a formidable task. This was made all the more difficult by the general fatigue of the Expeditionary Corps and the departure of many of its more experienced senior officers. Inevitably, the strategy adopted by the new general followed familiar lines: hold presently controlled areas, continue to increase and strengthen the Vietnamese National Army, and strike at Viet Minh main force units to hurt them to the point where the communist command would agree to negotiate an end to the struggle.

In mid-1953 the Viet Minh mustered 125,000 regular troops supported by 75,000 regional and 150,000 popular forces. The French had 175,000 men in their Expeditionary Corps plus 55,000 native auxiliaries. The armies of the Associated States totalled 226,000: the Vietnamese National Army, representing 151,000 regulars and 48,000 auxiliaries, the Royal Khmer Army having a strength of 13,000, and an equal number making up the National Laotian Army. Ten per cent. of the Expeditionary Corps was dedicated to mobile strike forces. These included eight parachute battalions, seven combat commands (Groupes Mobiles), and two amphibious groups. The air component had 336 aircraft organized into four F8F Bearcat fighter, two B-26 bomber and three C-47 transport squadrons. The brown water navy comprised eight naval assult divisions.

These forces, while apparently substantial, were barely equal to their many responsibilities. It continued to be necessary for the French as well as the Viet Minh to select with care where to direct their offensive efforts. By the end of summer, French intelligence had noted that the Viet Minh were building roads in the northwest uplands toward Dien Bien Phu, presumably to establish a base to support operations in Laos. The French decided to evacuate Na San in favor of organizing themselves in Dien Bien Phu to disrupt Viet Minh plans more effectively. At the same time, the French launched Operations 'Mouette' and 'Pelican' in the northern delta. These were intended to discourage the Viet Minh from the ambitious adventures they had been contemplating in that same area.

The French move into Dien Bien Phu in November 1953 was not enthusiastically supported by all concerned. The air force, in particular, was disturbed by the distance between its air bases and the objective, the paucity of air resources in the theater and, significantly, in the magnitude of the requirements to support other scheduled operations. Because of these difficulties and priorities, the air force had to limit the air resupply for Dien Bien Phu to sixty tons per day. Some ground force officers also questioned the military utility of Dien Bien Phu on the premise that its possession could not really prevent the Viet Minh from moving into Laos. Further, there was some question over whether the place was to serve as a base to support offensive operations or politico-military activity.

Even as the French were moving into Dien Bien Phu, their intelligence was reporting the movement of Viet Minh units in the vicinity. That news was disquieting, but still General Navarre appeared confident and his staff looked at Dien Bien Phu as another Na San — a stronghold against which Viet Minh battle forces would expend themselves uselessly. Indeed, such was the level of confidence, that even with reports of severe clashes between French and Viet Minh units near Lai Chau and just outside of Dien Bien Phu itself, no change was made in the plans for Operation 'Atlante'. This was a large scale amphibious operation scheduled to begin on 20 January 1954 and continue over a period of six months. Its purpose was to clear the coastal zone between Tourane and Nha Trang which was Viet Minh infested. The first phase of Operation 'Atlante' alone required twenty-five infantry battalions. In this context, Dien Bien Phu clearly was of secondary importance.

At the end of 1953, Ho Chi Minh had proclaimed in the press his readiness to discuss an end to hostilities. General Giap argued that a major victory would strengthen the communist hand if, in fact, negotiations were to be undertaken. A major effort against Dien Bien Phu was clearly indicated. The preparations for this offensive did not pass without notice of the French, already alerted by their earlier intelligence reports. But, General Navarre refused to evacuate the position in the face of the communist build-up, as his instructions allowed. Instead, he added three battalions to the garrison,

Moroccan troops of the 1st Battalion, 4th Regiment move forward against light resistance in operations in the Phu Ly area of Tonkin, August 1953. No matter how well mechanized a force is, there comes a time when the infantry takes to its feet. This was more often true for the troops of the French Expeditionary Corps during the Indochina War who were called upon to fight in a difficult terrain and exhausting climate. (ECPA)

47

Rear Admiral Jean Marie Querville, French Navy, Commander French Naval Forces Tonkin, October 1954 with Lt Col. Victor Croizat (USMC). This photograph was taken while awaiting arrival of French Navy ships sent by the Admiral to pick up Vietnamese catholic refugees off the coast of Bui Chu and Phat Diem provinces. Denied transit to the Haiphong perimeter by the communist authorities, they had put to sea on whatever they could find that would float. Learning of this, Admiral Querville immediately ordered his ships to move in as close to shore as possible to save these poor people. When reminded that his ships were entering territorial waters without permission, he turned a deaf ear and ordered his ships to continue their inshore operations.

General J. Lawton Collins visits a refugee camp in Haiphong in November 1954 in the company of Governor Le Quang Luat. The author, the escorting officer, was at that time commander of the MAAG detachment in Haiphong and concerned with the U.S. military participation in the evacuation effort.

General J. Lawton Collins (with hat), ambassador to Vietnam in 1954, came to North Vietnam to observe the status of the evacuation of the French military forces and refugees. He was received by Major General René Cogny, commanding French Union Forces in the Zone d'Operations de Tonkin and M. Le Quang Luat, the last governor of North Vietnam.

Lt Col. Blanchet (facing the camera), Regulateur General at Haiphong in October 1954; he was the representative of the Commander of French Forces in Indochina on all matters relating to the evacuation of the French Expeditionary Corps, indigenous levies and refugees. The officer with his head turned toward camera is Commandant de Champeau, representing the Base d'Operations de Tonkin, the principal base organization in North Vietnam. Haiphong served as the major evacuation port from Tonkin.

French liaison officers aboard AGC Estes, the flagship of the amphibious force of the Seventh Fleet in Baie d'Along, in October 1954.

French naval personnel take a break after returning from a long coastal patrol of North Vietnamese waters.

Opposite
Embarkation of refugees on a French Navy LSM at La Briqueterie, in October 1954. Refugees destined for Saigon on U.S. ships were moved from reception centers in Haiphong to an embarkation site at La Briqueterie where they were loaded on French Navy landing ships for a four hour trip to the Baie d'Along where they transferred to U.S. ships for the move to Saigon.

U.S. Navy medical personnel spraying refugees prior to embarkation, in October 1954.

bringing its total to 12,000 men, and decided to make a stand. In the final days of the year the Viet Minh completed their encirclement of the position and the scene was set for the last tragedy of the Indochina War. Navarre, like Giap, believed that a military victory would give a better position at a peace conference.

In January 1954 Operation 'Atlante' was launched as planned against the coast of Annam. At the same time, the communist command made diversionary thrusts against Thakhek, a Laotian town on the Mekong River, and in the upland plateau area. Then, at the end of January began the probes of the Dien Bien Phu position where, in time, Giap was to engage 80,000 men supported over a single line of communications more than 500 kilometers long.

As the tempo of battle intensified and the press reported on the vigor of the communist initiatives, the French government became increasingly alarmed. Defense Minister Pleven was promptly dispatched to Indochina in February to investigate and report. After visiting all battlefronts in a nineteen day action-packed tour, Pleven returned to Paris where he recommended that France include the settlement of the Indochina War on the agenda of the Four Power (U.S., U.S.S.R., U.K., and France) Conference that was to meet in Geneva that April. The government accepted the recommendation.

The reactions of the Associated States to the peace initiative varied. Cambodia was in favor, but the government of Laos resigned and a new one was formed. In Vietnam there was great internal dissension among peace factions, one calling for the full independence of Vietnam outside of the French Union before coming to the peace talks. Bao Dai, in contrast, advocated the intensification of the struggle against the communists and called for greater firmness rather than a negotiated peace.

On the battlefronts of Indochina, events unfolded with an internal inertia that made them appear independent of the political activity prevailing. On 13 March the Viet Minh offensive began in earnest. While Viet Minh artillery pounded the French positions at Dien Bien Phu, communist commandos struck at air bases in the Hanoi-Haiphong sector and destroyed twenty-two aircraft. Then, at Dien Bien Phu, after five hours of violent action the first position fell; the second quickly followed. The French, surprised at the power and concentration of the Viet Minh, failed to react with their accustomed vigor. On 17 March, the Viet Minh paused to resupply and regroup. They then returned to the attack where they systematically overran each of the French positions one after the other. Finally, on 7 May, the remnants of the garrision surrendered.

Dien Bien Phu cost the Viet Minh 8000 dead. French killed and missing totalled under 3000, but the wounded and survivors all passed into captivity. The French losses, amounting to seventeen battalions of infantry were serious but not decisive. What was decisive was the loss of the will to fight. There were battles to follow Dien Bien Phu, but these were little more than tactical actions to improve positions. The war had, in fact, already ended when the official ceasefire agreed in Geneva went into effect in the north on 27 July and in the south on 11 August.

The Union forces engaged against the Viet Minh in the Indochina War included 175,000 men in the Expeditionary Corps, and some 55,000 auxiliaries. In addition, the armies of the Associated States numbered 226,000 of which 200,000 were Vietnamese; the rest were equally divided between Cambodians and Laotians. Within the Expeditionary Corps there were 75,000 Europeans

Viet Minh Army troops entering Hanoi in 1954.

(French and Legionnaires), 50,000 Africans and 50,000 Indochinese, most of whom were Vietnamese.

The Geneva Accords provided 300 days for the opposing military forces to be regrouped north and south of a 'provisional demarcation line', the 17th parallel. Civilians could elect to move in like fashion during the same period. The French, uncertain how well the communists would respect the Accords, maintained covering forces in position until the final departure in early 1955.

In compliance with the Agreement, the French airlifted 147,000 people and moved 350,000 more personnel, plus 15,000 vehicles and 400,000 tons of equipment and supplies, by sea. U.S. Navy Seventh Fleet and MSTS ships evacuated 310,846 people, 8135 vehicles and 68,787 tons of equipment and supplies. The French figures include personnel of the Expeditionary Corps, indigenous military units and dependants, and civilian refugees. U.S. figures represent primarily refugees.

5

The French Brown Water Navy:
Organization

The exceptional difficulties encountered by the opposing military forces in the Indochina War were matched by their exceptional courage and resourcefulness. The performance of the communist troops, completely without air support and possessed only of rudimentary logistics and communications was truly remarkable. The tragedy is that these soldierly qualities should have served the ends of a despotism ruling by fear.

The French Expeditionary Corps and its indigenous auxiliaries are equally deserving of recognition for their military prowess. Those who may seek to attribute this to advantages in armaments, equipment, and supplies must be reminded that resources available seldom met requirements and that, for many of these troops, Indochina was an alien environment as difficult to master as the enemy that was native to it. Moreover, in response to ever-changing government directives, the war had to be waged for often contradictory objectives, within a complex and uncertain political climate,

and under a cumbersome command system. It is noteworthy that despite such circumstances the Indochina War should have enabled the development of the doctrinal basis for modern riverine warfare.

The innovativeness of the French is clearly revealed by the manner in which they adapted organizations and equipment of both the army and the navy to the peculiar requirements of the Indochinese theater of operations. As noted earlier, the main task of the Expeditionary Corps was to seek out and destroy the military organization of the communist Viet Minh. To do so, it had to maneuver and fight over vast coastal and deltaic areas criss-crossed by waterways and with few, if any, roads.

The French were well aware of the utility of airborne forces in such terrain. They had built up their parachutist strength of some 5000 men in 1949 to fourteen battalions in 1954; six of these in the Expeditionary Corps proper and the remainder in the armies of the Associated States. These units had participated in 150 operations in the course of the war, but most of these had been in a supporting rôle because there were never enough transport aircraft and crews for anything else. The French, in fact, were never able to muster a lift for more than two battalions.

The inadequacy of resources was even greater where helicopters were concerned. The operational flexibility that the helicopter can provide in difficult terrain was well appreciated but, in 1952, there were only a dozen machines in Indochina. When the war ended in 1954, there still were less than fifty. These were too few for anything more than medical evacuations and occasional liaison missions. There were plans to increase the numbers of helicopters greatly in 1955,

Air drop of emergency supplies during Hoa Binh offensive in Tonkin in November 1951. (ECPA)

One of the first helicopter medevac missions flown during Operation 'Normandie' in support of units of the 1st Legion Regiment engaged in the Plain of Reeds in June 1950. The French were well aware of the importance of aviation support for ground operations but lacked the means needed to exploit this capability. Helicopters would have been particularly valuable; there were only two in Indochina in 1950 and only eight had been added by 1952. The army-air force mixed helicopter group that was to have 50 helicopters actually only received 28 by the time the Indochina War had ended. As a result, the French used whatever means there were available and worked their parachute units particularly hard. (ECPA)

French Navy Grumman Goose amphibian aircraft used for surveillance and medevac during Operation 'Domino' in support of riverine assault operations in Cochinchina 1952. (ECPA)

By the time of Dien Bien Phu, the larger Sikorsky helicopters were available. These, while still few, were used for medavac as shown but were also used for rescue and the first attempts at tactical operations. (ECPA)

but these were not implemented. The effort was not wasted, however, for it soon found application in the Algerian War just beginning.

With only limited airborne capabilities, the French had to depend on more conventional equipment, much of it left over from World War II, to provide the mobility required. The utilization of such equipment and its integration into specialized organizations began early in the Indochina War. The process continued to evolve throughout that conflict.

Three branches of the army — transportation, engineers, and armor — were involved in brown water operations from the beginning. The Transportation Corps adapted quickly, for it had used local craft in the conquest of Tonkin toward the end of the nineteenth century. This experience, albeit long past, was repeated in the early days of the Indochina War to meet transportation requirements in the ports of Saigon, Tourane (Danang) and Haiphong. Still, it took several years before an effective river transport organization emerged.

In 1948 some fifty amphibious trucks (DUKW) were procured from U.S. Army surplus stocks in the Philippines. These were worn and proved to be of little use. They were soon discarded. Then, beginning in 1951, LCMs began arriving. These were formed into two river transport companies of four platoons each. Each platoon had eight LCMs, one officer and eighty men. The LCMs were very reliable boats and served well throughout the war. As eventually deployed, there were three platoons assigned in Tonkin, and one based in Hue to serve the needs in Annam. In Cochinchina there were three platoons based in Saigon and a fourth in Phom Penh.

These army LCM units, often confused in reports with similar navy units, were used mainly for routine supply and personnel transport missions. Each LCM could carry 30 tons in stages of 75 to 200 kilometers. In Cochinchina they provided regular service between Saigon and Cap Sainte Jacques (Vung Tau), Kratie, Mytho and Phnom Penh. The army LCMs also were used in combat operations. The LCM was protected by 15 mm. armor and carried two machine-guns and a grenade launcher. They could

navigate alone in insecure areas, although in such environments they were most often accompanied by patrol boats able to reconnoiter passages and provide additional fire support as necessary. When they participated in tactical operations as such, the LCMs were integrated into a naval river force.

The Engineer Corps included among its many tasks those of developing river ports and beaching sites as well as furnishing river crossing services and combat engineer support during operations on the waterways. To meet these latter responsibilities, two types of companies were organized within the general reserve units. The first was a ferry boat service company. Because the bridging of rivers exceeding 250 meters in width was not feasible, the engineers were tasked with providing the requisite ferry services. For this purpose they used heavy pontoon barges powered by large outboard motors. These proved generally satisfactory, but, where currents were swift, it became necessary to call on the navy for their LCTs (landing craft, tank). The second type of special engineer unit created for Indochina service was an armored boat company with heavy engineer equipment used to support tactical riverine operations.

The Armored Corps proved particularly innovative in adapting itself to the demanding environment. An early adaptation was the conversion of some reconnaissance units for brown water operations. When these units were deployed into delta areas they replaced their wheeled and tracked vehicles with boats, generally STCAN/FOM patrol boats, with which they carried on their normal tasks of patrol, escort, liaison, tactical maneuver and emergency resupply. Like the LCM units of the army, these river cavalry elements generally operated independently. They were also available to escort LCMs or to join in larger tactical operations as part of a naval river force.

The army armored forces were also quick to discover the usefulness of light tracked cargo carriers which they called 'crabs'. These amphibious vehicles, originally conceived for the movement of supplies in snow country, had been used in the Pacific War at Iwo Jima in Febru-

ary 1945, where they were known to the American Marines as 'weasels'. This 2-ton amphibian had little carrying capacity, but its low track pressure and floatability made it highly maneuverable in swampy areas. When they first arrived in Indochina, these vehicles were used for reconnaissance and flanking or encirclement operations in the Mekong delta, earning an excellent reputation in tactical operations. Because of their high mobility in marshy terrain, the 'crabs' invariably outdistanced accompanying infantry. And since they were lightly armed, without armor, and their tracks were relatively fragile, they were put out of action with little enemy effort. They proved particularly vulnerable when used individually, as they were in the Plain of Reeds, where their carcasses soon littered the landscape.

This problem was first addressed in 1948 by grouping the 'crabs' into a two-company battalion wherein the vehicles were used together to gain mutual fire support. Each company with its 33 vehicles had considerable firepower: 30 machine-guns, six recoilless 57 mm guns and three 60 mm mortars. Then it was found that combat effectiveness was improved further by assigning one platoon of infantry to each company of 'crabs'. These measures progressively reduced vehicle losses. However, a platoon of infantry was too light to sustain combat and too heavy to be transported easily in the 'crabs', whose carrying capacity did not allow for the assignment of more than one platoon of infantry for protection. This was inadequate and the vulnerability of the M29C units remained high.

Attention was then turned to a larger tracked cargo vehicle, the LVT(4), of which the French had obtained a number. This particular model was first used in the landing on Saipan in June 1944. It was a member of the family of tracked amphibious vehicles that, beginning with the LVT(1) used on Guadalcanal in 1942, had made it possible to land troops across reefs restricting access to many Pacific islands.

The 16-ton LVT(4) could carry thirty equipped troops or equivalent cargo. It was fitted with a stern ramp for easy access and mounted three .30 and one .50 caliber machine-guns. Its track pressure was considerably greater than that of the M29C; still, it could maneuver in and out of waterways with acceptable ease. Another version of the same vehicle, the LVT(A)(4) was fitted with an open turret housing a 75 mm howitzer. The availability of these vehicles with their complementary capabilities led to the organization of two Amphibious Groups. As constituted at the end of the Indochina war, each of these comprised two companies of M29C, three companies of infantry mounted in LVT(4)s and one platoon of six cannon firing LVT(A)(4)s. The M29C units provided the scouting and rapid maneuver capability, the LVT(4)s deployed their infantry into favorable tactical dispositions and the 75s of the LVT(A)4 supported the action.

The Amphibious Groups normally mounted out for combat operations with three days of supplies. They also had sufficient communications and staff to form two task forces. They were, thus, exceptionally versatile and mobile organizations including, as they did, their own reconnaissance, maneuver and fire-support elements under a single command. These Groups, moreover, were easily embarked in amphibious shipping and could be landed from the sea at virtually any place along the coast.

The principal limitation of this unusual brown water organization was in the weakness of the tracks of the 'crabs'. The LVTs, although capable of greater performance, were not without mechanical vulnerabilities either. Because of these problems and to reduce wear on tracks, suspension systems and transmissions, it was necessary to move the tracked vehicles from their base parks to assembly areas in the combat zone by trucks or tank transporters. There was also a difference in the ease with which these two types of vehicles performed in delta country. The 'crabs' had very little track pressure and could move over soft ground where the heavier LVT(4) and LVT(A)(4) would belly down. They also differed in their ability to crawl out of a waterway on to a bank or dike. Thus, it was essential to plan the deployment and tactical employment of these units with careful regard for the particular limitations of their tracked vehicles. When

this was done, the units proved themselves immensely valuable and generally caused the enemy heavy casualties.

The Amphibious Groups enjoyed exceptional tactical mobility in coastal and riverine environments. Their strategic mobility was limited, however, since the amphibious vehicles had to be transported to the area of operations. Further, their mechanical weakness made them unsuitable for routine operations, such as patrolling, which had to be carried out on a continuing basis. There was never any question, therefore, but that the boat in its many guises would retain its singular importance in Indochina. This, in turn, assured the navy an important rôle in the war.

The need of a true brown water navy was demonstrated soon after General Leclerc arrived in Saigon in 1945. The British commander, General Gracey, had orders to receive the surrender of the Japanese but not to become embroiled in peace-keeping. This task he was pleased to allow to the French. But, because shipping was in short supply, the French were slow to return to Indochina. In the meanwhile, the security situation in the south was deteriorating rapidly. On

The amphibious cargo carrier M29C was first used on Iwo Jima during World War II. This 2-ton vehicle was able to carry only 500 kgs, including a crew of two, but was able to operate in swampy terrain. The Americans called the vehicle 'weasel'. The vehicle shown here was assigned to the 1st U.S. Marine Division in Korea in August 1952. The French made extensive use of the M29C in Indochina where they were called 'crabs'. (USMC)

21 September, General Gracey was compelled to declare martial law and seize the public buildings in Saigon. Then, on 12 October, General Gracey had British troops join the French outside the city in a move to restore order in the nearby countryside. At that time, some two months after the Japanese capitulation, General Leclerc had only 4500 French troops. Still, the situation called for action and General Leclerc responded. He decided to strike out and regain control of Cochinchina using the forces available. This, he decided to do by seizing key population centers and gaining control over the mouths of the Mekong River.

His first objective, the city of Mytho 60 kilometers south of Saigon, was to be taken by an armored ground force. A navy commando was to make its way to

The LVT(4) was the third type of tracked amphibian to appear during World War II. It was fitted with a ramp aft which allowed it to carry light vehicles or up to 30 troops. The French used these as the troop lift in their amphibious groups in Indochina. The LVT shown was with the 5th U.S. Marine Division and was photographed in February 1945 during an advance shortly after landing on Iwo Jima. (USMC)

The LVT(A)(4) was an 18-ton amphibious vehicle mounting a 75mm howitzer in an open turret. First used in the invasion of Saipan in 1944, it later appeared in Indochina where the French assigned six such vehicles per amphibious group. The vehicle was able to carry 100 rounds of 75 mm ammunition and 400 rounds for its single .50 caliber machine-gun. (USN)

The wide ranging combat engagements that signalled the start of the Indochina War quickly demonstrated the need for specialized vehicles to cope with the difficult terrain characteristic of the delta areas. One of the first such vehicles pressed into service was the amphibious truck known as the DUKW. The French procured 50 of these vehicles from the U.S. Army for use in Indochina in 1948. These 6-ton wheeled vehicles could carry 2.5 tons of cargo or 25 troops and travelled at 5 knots in the water. They were useful for routine transportation tasks on land, but their cross-country mobility was less satisfactory and they proved to be of limited use in the delta areas of Vietnam. The DUKW shown is from the 2/515 Transport Company operating in the Phu Ly area of Tonkin in April 1951. (ECPA)

An LCM of the French Army Transportation Corps in Tonkin resupplies a post of the Foreign Legion 2/13 Demi-Brigade on the Black River near Hoa Binh, in 1952. Use of rivercraft was made necessary because the Viet Minh had cut Route Coloniale 6 in 1952. (ECPA)

STCAN/FOM patrol boats of the French 4th Dragoons investigate a river bank in the Mekong Delta in 1952. (ECPA)

the same location by water. The army moved out at dawn on 15 October but soon encountered obstacles, road cuts and shattered bridges. By nightfall it had reached only halfway to its objective. The navy commando, embarked in a British LCI (Landing Craft, Infantry), had left at the same time and moved along without incident. It reached

Mytho at 0230 the morning of the 16th and, having gained surprise, it soon controlled the town. The army column, moving overland, arrived the following evening. General Leclerc recognized the significance of this experience and thenceforth used elements of the Far East Naval Brigade, formed in December 1944 for service in the Pacific War, to seize other key population centers in the delta.

This brigade was the navy's contribution to the Expeditionary Corps and was organized around a regiment of 'marines'. Once in Indochina, the brigade was reorganized into two river flotillas and a navy parachute commando; the regiment of 'marines' remained in reduced form as an 'amphibious assault force'.

In mid-November 1945 the Viet Minh slaughtered nineteen French sailors in an ambush on the water route between Mytho and Saigon. They were to repeat this tactic often. They became equally skilled in the use of controlled mines and in attacks on river posts and anchorages, sometimes using swimmers for the purpose. The French responded to these events by changing the organization of their brown water navy forces.

In early 1946 the brigade was broken down into two separate elements. One element, sent to Tonkin, included the 1st River Flotilla with some thirty assorted river craft. The 2nd River Flotilla with some sixty similar types of boats remained in the south. Then on 1 January 1947, the brigade ceased to be a subordinate entity within the Expeditionary Corps and became the Naval Amphibious Force, Indochina, under the admiral commanding French naval forces in the Far East. The two-element organization was retained but under new designations.

The Northern Group was made up of the 1st Amphibious Flotilla which included river and coastal bases in Tonkin, the base of Tourane (Danang) in Annam, and five commandos. The Southern Group, made up of the 2nd Amphibious Flotilla, was similarly organized but included only two Commandos; its bases were in the Mekong River delta of Cochinchina, at Phnon Penh in Cambodia, and in Laos. The dinassaut organizations (naval assault divisions) that soon followed represented a natural evolutionary process and appeared as further organizational and operational refinements to the peculiarities of the riverine environment.

The dinassaut comprised different types of craft corresponding to specific functions; command/fire support, transportation, and patrol/minesweeping. The dinassaut could combine these resources as needed for a given task and environment. This represented a highly flexible operational concept and explains why the dinassauts served with little change during the Indochina War, continued later as river assault groups in the Vietnamese Navy, and eventually became the river assault squadrons used by the Americans in the Vietnam War.

The majority of ships and craft used in the dinassauts had originally been designed for amphibious operations in World War II. They had little or no armor and only relatively light armament. For these craft to serve on inland waters they had to be armored to withstand the shock of surprise encounters at short ranges. They also needed substantial armament to deliver promptly the heavy volume of fire to counter an ambush. Armament, moreover, had to include a mix of high and flat trajectory weapons to ensure that all types of targets along the waterways and over the river banks could be taken under fire.

The French were remarkably successful in adapting the available material to these particular imperatives of brown water warfare. They were no less successful at devising appropriate tactics. These exploited the diverse capabilities of the dinassaut's resources and, whenever possible, made use of air and of shore-based artillery. Air was seldom readily at hand, however, and the use of artillery depended upon its reach.

For command and fire support the French preferred landing ships such as LSI (landing ship, infantry); LSIL (landing ship, infantry, light) and LSSL (landing ship, support, light). These had the communications suited to the needs of a force commander, heavy weapons such as 3-inch and 40 mm. cannon, and a high bridge. This last was very important for it permitted the force commander to maintain visual contact with much of his force when underway and to direct the fire of his shipboard weapons personally.

The dinassaut had one such ship. For specific operations two could be assigned but this was rare. In cases where waters were restricted the command and fire-support functions were performed by LCMs (landing craft, medium), separately modified for these rôles. Command LCMs were armored and armed with 20 mm cannon, 81 mm mortars and .50 and .30 caliber machine-guns. The LCM monitors used for fire support were similarly armed but also had a 40 mm cannon. Some of these had tank turrets with guns fitted forward instead of the 40 mm cannon. There were even some equipped with flamethrowers and rocket launchers but these never saw combat. The French found the monitors useful but would

The LSIL was used as a fire support and command ship by the French and later the Vietnamese.

59

have preferred the larger LCT (landing craft, tank) for the rôle because they were powerful and could be heavily armed. But, all LCTs were needed for logistic tasks and very few were spared to become fire support craft. The transport capability of a dinassaut was represented by two LCMs and four of the smaller LCVPs (landing craft, vehicle/personnel). These all were armored and armed with 20 mm cannon and a mix of .30 and .50 caliber machine-guns. This lift capability was modest but could be augmented to embark up to a battalion of infantry for the larger landing assault operations.

The patrol element originally included one harbor patrol type boat. Then, when the mine threat developed, a sweeping capability was added. At this same time the navy introduced the STACN/FOM boat. These were eleven meter boats built of steel with a V-shaped hull and capable of ten knots. They were armed with .30 and .50 caliber machine-guns. These boats were generally reliable and saw extensive service. The fact their hulls were resistant to mine blast damage was a great advantage when they were used as minesweepers.

Movement on inland waters in a combat zone requires boats with characteristics comparable to those of ground vehicles engaged in like circumstances on land. But, to remain afloat and able to maneuver made it necessary to limit the armor and armament of boats to something less than the threat required. Even so, the modifications needed for survival and combat made dinassaut boats unsuited to offshore operations. Landing ships with bridges and deck weapons protected by armor were top heavy and unstable in the swells of the South China Sea. The smaller river craft were even less seaworthy. These limitations made the coastal patrols and amphibious operations dependent upon the resources of the Far East Naval Division, the blue water component of the French Navy Forces, Far East.

Yet another factor affecting the use of dinassauts was that they could range widely over the interconnected waterways of the deltas of Cochinchina and Tonkin but not over those in Annam. The inland waters there were shallow and movement from one waterway to another required going out to sea. Sepa-

The STCAN/FOM patrol boat of French design was a very effective river craft. It was 11 meters in length, 13 tons in weight, and capable of 9 knots.

rate small boat units were deployed in Annam accordingly. Finally, as the combat capabilities of the Viet Minh improved, it became increasingly unwise to engage in offensive operations with only one dinassaut, even when it was reinforced. River task forces drawn from several dinassauts augmented by boats from the army and navy were organized for major actions.

Viewed from the perspective of years of warfare, the dinassauts performed well and represented a sound organizational and operational concept. But, they were limited in their combat power and radius of action. They were true brown water formations. Blue water tasks as well as much of the activity in the coastal interface zone between brown and blue waters necessarily devolved upon the conventional navy.

6

The French Brown Water Navy:
Operations

A major concern of the French from the moment of their return to Indochina was to maintain their freedom of movement. This required control over essential lines of communications and was accomplished by the organization of security posts linked by regular patrols, the whole supported by mobile reserves held ready at key positions for immediate intervention. This process was costly in men and equipment and was applied primarily to safeguard major road nets. Movement on inland waters remained relatively insecure and soon came to require escort and minesweeping services for many routine logistic purposes; in short, it became necessary to organize convoys. This naval character of riverine operations appeared from the very beginning and remained in evidence all through the war.

The tactics of the French brown river navy began to evolve with the very first efforts in 1945 to clear the area around Saigon and the river route to Mytho. The 'marines' under Commander Pontchardier, having established their utility in the seizure of Mytho, moved on to take Vinh Long and, on 30 October 1945, they seized Cantho. Forty-two other landing operations were needed to clear the central delta of communist elements. In these operations the technique was evolved of using boat gun fire to fix the enemy while an embarked infantry force was landed to flank and encircle him. This experience confirmed the striking importance of heavy fire power combined with an embarked infantry maneuver element.

Soon after the formal beginning of the Indochina War in December, 1946, it became necessary to open the Hanoi-Haiphong road. It was decided to use a river force to clear the river to the midpoint of Hai Duong. The force used included two LCTs embarking one Foreign Legion infantry battalion; two LCMs embarking a light tank platoon; one LCM loaded with the tracked 'crabs'; five LCA, (landing craft) carrying engineer units with the equipment needed to repair bridges and the road bed; and one LCS (landing craft support) to provide fire support.

The force moved out at first light on 21 December and made its first landing at 0800. After clearing the area around the landing site it moved on and made a second landing at mid-day. A third landing was made twenty-four hours later and a fourth at 1900 on the 23rd. The fifth and final landing at Hai Duong proper was made on the 24th. There were several violent actions along the way but none of a critical nature. Viet Minh documents captured later revealed that the French had been expected, but by road. The use of the river had gained the element of surprise for the French and had denied the communists the time to react and impede their passage.

Another operation during this same period involved the relief of Nam Dinh. This northern town is on a canal a short distance from the Red River and had been isolated soon after hostilities began. The French garrison and civilian groups had been compressed into several perimeters; the former had to be reinforced and resupplied while the latter group had to be evacuated. The French decided to drop a parachute unit near the town to seize a landing site on the canal. A Foreign Legion rifle company reinforced with armor and engineer elements would then land and clear the way for a motor convoy that was also embarked. The trucks, preloaded with ammunition and supplies, would reinforce the troops in the town and return the civilians to the boats that would remove them to a safe haven.

As it happened, the first drop of pathfinders alerted the Viet Minh, with the result that nine of the ten transport aircraft that followed with the first assault group were hit by automatic weapons fire. This threw off the timing of the parachute drop so that when the river force appeared off the landing site at 0620 as planned, they were greeted by hostile fire rather than by friendly troops.

With twenty-two men hit in the first few minutes of their arrival, the landing force commander would have been justified in withdrawing. Instead, he immediately ordered the force to land on the opposite bank and set up a base of fire to support the parachutists who were even then fighting to reach the landing site. The combined action from both banks succeeded. With the landing site secured, the river force crossed the river and completed the operation as originally planned. By 1700 the civilian evacuees had been re-embarked and the river force retired. What could easily have been a disaster ended well, thanks to a quick thinking officer who knew how to exploit the maneuverability of his boats.

In this same general area there occurred later yet another typical dinassaut operation. In early February 1948, French intelligence had reported that an important Viet Minh installation was located on the Day River about 10 kms north of Glan Khau. It was decided to raid this installation with a dinassaut based at Nam Dinh 65 kms by river from this enemy concentration. The approach would need to be through Viet Minh territory.

On the evening of 1 February 1948, the Nam Dinh dinassaut, composed of four LCMs and two LCAs (ex-British craft similar to US LCVPs) with embarked marines, left the base and set its speed to reach the target area on the following morning. By making the movement under darkness a degree of surprise was attained. Early the next morning, the landing party swept through the enemy installations against light opposition, leaving behind a path of destruction.

Supporting Operations. *In any firefight, the side with the greatest firepower has a decided advantage. The problem is how to obtain heavy fire when needed. The LVT(A)(4) with its 75 mm howitzer in an open turret was the standard heavy support within the army's amphibious groups. Still, the navy's 40 mm, rapid firing cannon on the LSSL, LSIL, and monitors was also much appreciated, and marrying it to the amphibian tractor seemed worth the effort. The other solution used as often as not was to embark artillery units in the river assault boats. In matters of transport, the high maneuverability of the 'crab' in swamps was well known. Unfortunately the track of the light amphibious vehicle was fragile. This meant that the 'crab' had to be transported to its operational area in standard 2½-ton trucks.*

During Operation 'Amphibie' conducted in the Nam Dinh area of Tonkin in March 1952 a 40 mm cannon mounted in an LVT(4) was taken along. (ECPA)

In December 1950 Dinassaut 3 conducted a clearing operation against a village in Tonkin using Vietnamese troops supported by a battery of French artillery. Note the winter overcoats worn by French troops. (ECPA)

Opposite
A search and destroy operation was conducted in the Tra Vinh area of Cochinchina in October 1950 using the 'crab' light amphibious vehicle for reconnaissance purposes. (ECPA)

The French dinassaut commander anticipated a quick enemy reaction, most probably in the nature of an ambush during his withdrawal either while his troops were returning to their boats, or later as the boats proceeded downstream to their base. To meet the first threat, the landing force was instructed to return to the beach as quickly as possible in the hope that the enemy would not have time to collect himself and take position. This was successfully done.

After spending the night of 2 February off Gian Khau, the dinassaut began to move down river to Nam Dinh. In expectation of an ambush, a plan had been developed by which the LCMs and LCAs would be divided equally into two columns. One LCA preceded each of these columns by about 500 yards and stayed close inshore to detect enemy mines controlled from the banks. In the event of ambush, instructions were clear. One of the two LCMs in each column would immediately close the nearest bank and debark its troops who, under cover of the dinassaut's fire power would push inland against the enemy. The LCAs would perform the same maneuver and their troops would land against the enemy flank and rear. Meanwhile the remaining LCM in each of the columns would provide fire support but retain its troops in reserve.

This simple plan was soon put to use. At noon, the convoy was hit with a heavy concentration of 37 mm machine-gun, mortar, and small arms fire. On the north bank, the French counter-attack completely disorganized and then trapped the communist forces who lost 105 dead. On the south bank the counter-action did not proceed as well, due primarily to the breakdown of the LCA in this column and the need for it to be taken in tow by one of the LCMs. This LCA was sunk early in the action, but the landing party from the LCM forced the communists to withdraw from their positions, leaving behind several dead and some 60 mm mortars. Although the enemy on the south bank escaped, this action, which lasted only 20 minutes, proved tactically sound. French losses during the raid were only one LCA lost and one man wounded.

It should not be assumed from the foregoing that the French Navy was always able to defeat the ambush problem. On the contrary, many waterways had to be abandoned because of enemy activity. However, the major waterways were generally kept open, although at an ever increasing cost in personnel and *matériel*. Neither should it be assumed that raids of the nature just described were a main feature of the river war. Such raids were frequent, but so were operations conducted in close coordination with major land offensives. Finally, the dinassauts

French amphibious units engaged in Operation 'Crachin' in Ninh Giang area of Tonkin on 12 February 1952.

Right
A troop-carrying LVT(4) clearing a low dike separating two rice fields. Note the 75 mm recoilless rifle forward of the cab. (ECPA)

Opposite right
A tactical column in the Tra Vinh area, Cochinchina, showing a troop-carrying LVT(4) in the lead followed by two 'Crabs'. (ECPA)

Below
A 'Crab' climbing a steep dike from a rice field. The vehicle is unarmoured and has a light machine-gun. Note the man in the rear with the radio set. (ECPA)

could be as effectively coordinated in a defensive rôle as in offensive operations.

These early operations confirmed that the brown water navy was well suited to offensive actions. They also demonstrated that the success of riverine operations, which generally involved movements from one river base to another, was best assured when heavy fire power could be combined with an embarked maneuver element that could be landed to clear hostile barrier forces. Ground force units were also an essential part of a river base defense organization. Thus the dinassauts evolved as combat organizations whose effectiveness lay in their ability to balance the fire power of heavily armed boats with the maneuverablity of embarked infantry to the degree required to accomplish a wide range of missions. It was always highly desirable for the infantry with the dinassauts to have received specialized training in riverine operations. This requirement, of direct relevance to the combat effectiveness of the dinassauts, was less compelling in the case of infantry units assigned to the defense of river bases.

The French river forces were administered by the French Navy, but they nor-

mally operated within territorial zones under army control. One of the four dinassaut commanders in Tonkin reported that all boats in his zone had been placed under his (navy) control and that his river posts served as the coordinating centers for the conduct of routine river patrols, logistic and combat operations wherein army units were invariably involved. Such informal command arrangements worked well when resources were adequate and circumstances encouraged cooperation. However, this was seldom the case for shortages were universal and the prevalence of conflicting requirements lessened opportunities for collaboration. It was not always possible to obtain ground units to train for riverine operations and in some cases ground unit commanders looked upon the dinassauts as more suited to supply than to combat operations.

The dinassauts at first had French Navy commandos as organic elements. These were later replaced by Vietnamese units who performed exceptionally well. Still, it was never possible to assign large battalion-sized units to a dinassaut permanently. This would have significantly improved dinassaut capabilities in the

systematic clearing of large areas by establishing a network of temporary bases from which boat patrols could radiate. Such operations were carried out with attached army units. But, such attachments were temporary and the troops involved often had little if any familiarity with boat operations. The French Navy repeatedly recommended the training of specialist ground force units to work with the dinassauts and eventually Vietnamese formations were so trained. These units never exceeded company size and their numbers were never commensurate with the requirement. Still, they proved highly effective and served, after the Indochina War, to form the Vietnamese Marine Corps, which was to flourish under the Americans.

In any discussion of the Indochina War the issue of resource availability inevitably arises. This is because the war was fought by both sides with limited means. The brown water navy in particular used a patch quilt of boats whose varied origins were matched by the modifications devised to improve their performance. Most of these boats, as already noted, were World War II landing ships and craft of American or British design.

All had to be adapted to local conditions and many had to be armored and armed. They also had to be made habitable for their crews, augmented to serve the additional weapons, who lived aboard except when the boats were at their rear bases.

The French did not encounter their enemy afloat. From this they concluded that the Viet Minh, while a remarkable infantryman, was not a sailor. Nonetheless, the French agreed that the communists made good use of controlled mines and swimmers. They were also masters of the use of terrain and camouflage and practised excellent fire discipline. They planned operations carefully and often combined attacks against river posts with ambushes to intercept relieving forces. They were equally adept at the organization of defenses along riverbanks.

In French eyes, the Viet Minh failed to take full advantage of the weaknesses of the French rivercraft and the difficulties in navigation. According to the French, the Viet Minh tended to limit the fields of fire of their heavy weapons to enhance their protection and camouflage. This reduced the time they could bear on moving targets and hence lowered the chances of a hit on a passing boat. The

French River Convoy Formation

Opening Group: An LCM monitor served as the column guide. Three two-boat sections of patrol-type minesweeping boats followed; a spare minesweeper was usually taken along to replace losses. The interval between the opening group and the main body was 200–300 meters. The usual distance maintained between large craft was 50 meters and between small craft 10–20 meters.

Support-Command Group: An LSSL or similar type ship, or two LCM monitors were used to lead the main body and provide fire support. When only one large ship was assigned, it also served as convoy command.

Transport Group: LCT, LCM or other types of cargo carrying craft were formed into a column. If the number of boats was large they were formed into two parallel columns; sometimes pairs of like craft such as LCMs were lashed together to facilitate control.

Alternate Command Group: When a second LSSL or equivalent was available it was stationed behind the transport group to provide fire support and serve as the convoy command ship (as illustrated). When three such vessels were available, the command ship was in the center.

Opening Group

LCM Monitor

Minesweepers

200-300 m

Support-Command Group

LSSL/LSIL

50 m

Transport Group

LCMs

10 m

10 m

50 m

Alternate Command Group

LSSL/LSIL

Concept of Operation: Actual distances between ships or craft in a convoy depended on the configuration of the river and the skill of the coxswains. Further, formations were closed up during night movements. When enemy forces were reported in the area, efforts were made to have air cover for the convoy. Under such conditions it was also the practice to fire on suspected enemy positions while the convoy continued to advance. In any event, if the convoy was fired upon it was normal practice to move ahead as quickly as possible to clear the danger zone. If time permitted and an infantry element was embarked, it was always better to land a maneuver element near the ambush site to destroy the enemy position.

Viet Minh also dispersed their weapons to lessen their vulnerability but then they were unable to mass their fire which significantly limited their effectiveness.

The Viet Minh did improve their tactics in time and the French suffered accordingly. Still, there were no significant changes in the operational concepts underlying the conduct of riverine operations throughout the Indochina War. These operations, as related, were intended to gain and maintain control over selected waterways, provide for the security of river bases and anchorages, and engage and destroy hostile forces by amphibious assault.

The tactics and techniques evolved for riverine operations were generally comparable to those used by armored ground forces moving overland on roads. The principal difference lay in the fact that a river force could not be camouflaged nor could the boats leave the river if attacked. This meant that it was seldom possible for river forces to gain tactical surprise. However, the power and mobility of such forces often enabled them to gain strategic surprise. In short, river forces added a further dimension to ground warfare. The French could maneuver their forces by land, water or air and the combining of these means of movement provided a high degree of operational flexibility. Even so, the preferred French tactic of encirclement failed at least as often as it succeeded in trapping significant Viet Minh forces.

The resources available determined the nature of operations. The most frequent were the patrols that were used to secure and control the major waterways. Patrols were conducted from river bases which were either permanent or temporary. A dinassaut would proceed from its home base to one of several advanced bases from which patrols, each made up of two or more boats, would be sent out daily. This pattern of activity, essentially of a routine nature, would be interrupted when large scale offensive operations were undertaken. Since these would usually require all available boats, area patrolling would have to be suspended. On occasion when operations involved more than one infantry battalion the dinassaut would require additional boats or two dinassauts would be assembled.

French River Assault Formation

Opening Group: An LCM monitor served as column guide. Three two-boat sections of patrol-type minesweepers followed; a spare minesweeper was usually taken along to replace losses. The opening group was followed by a shock group at a distance of 1000–1500 meters.

Shock Group: Two LSSLs or equivalent were used for fire support; one of these also served as the command ship embarking both the river force and landing force commanders. These ships were followed by the assault transportation element composed of up to four monitors and up to six armored LCMs, each with an infantry platoon or equivalent embarked. An LSSL or equivalent ship would be used as rear guide . The shock group was followed by the main body carrying the remainder of the landing force at a distance of about 1500 meters (not illustrated here). The concept of the assault operation using this shock group formation is described and illustrated on the following page, 68.

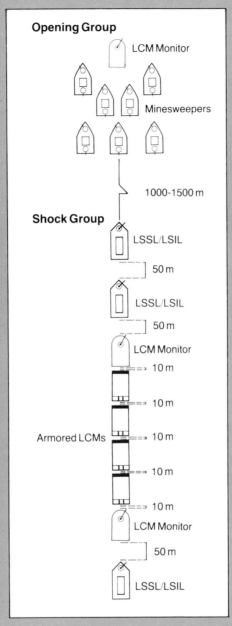

Opening Group

LCM Monitor

Minesweepers

1000-1500 m

Shock Group

LSSL/LSIL

50 m

LSSL/LSIL

50 m

LCM Monitor

10 m

10 m

Armored LCMs

10 m

10 m

10 m

LCM Monitor

50 m

LSSL/LSIL

Operations varied according to the mission, the nature of the threat, the numbers and types of boats available, the units to be embarked and their level of training, and the possibility of having air and artillery support. Despite these and other related variables, there were certain basic dispositions, derived from experience, that were used. First, all boats navigating in contested areas were formed into convoys. These comprised two groups; an 'opening' group made up of minesweeping and fire support boats, the latter usually LCM monitors. The main body embarking the troops or supplies being transported followed the opening group within two to three hundred meters. The main body included one or more fire support ships or craft (LSSL, LSIL or LCM monitors); the force commander normally took station on the larger of these at the head of the group. This position was particularly useful at night or when navigation was difficult since it gave the commander the best view of his force. It was also the best position from which to direct a response to hostile actions.

The distances between boats in the convoy depended on the skills of the coxswains but normally was held at two boat lengths. If large numbers of boats were present and the width of the waterway permitted, two parallel boat columns would be formed. This helped keep the formation together and multiplied the numbers of boats able to provide mutual supporting fire. Tight formations also were the rule for all night navigation.

The formation made up of two groups was used for logistic operations. Such convoys were concerned with reaching a given destination within a specified time. To that end uninterrupted movement was desired, and this, necessarily, had to limit the effectiveness of ambushes. When the presence of enemy forces was anticipated, observation aircraft were used to scout ahead of the convoy. Within the convoy, weapons were manned and predesignated counterambush assault units, if present, were positioned so as to be able to land on either bank on signal.

When speed was critical, the convoy would seek to force a passage past an ambush by saturating the site with a heavy volume of fire and moving ahead at full speed. This usually enabled the force to continue on its way but the tactic did little to hurt the enemy. The preferred tactic in the event of an encounter was to lay down a heavy fire on the enemy position while an infantry element was landed off his flank. Much of the success of this reaction depended on the volume of fire the boats could deliver and the complementary support that aviation and artillery could provide. If the fire was sufficient to immobilize the enemy, the landing and encirclement maneuver often worked well. If, however, the French fire left the Viet Minh some freedom of action, the latter usually managed to inflict painful casualties and withdraw before the French encirclement could be completed.

The Viet Minh were as quick to learn from experience as were the French. Ambushes, once set on only one side of a waterway, were soon organized on both banks. This caused the French to deploy forces against decoy positions or otherwise disperse their resources against multiple targets on opposing sides of the waterways. This also aggravated the

French River Assault Operation

Concept of Operation: (landing area on right of formation) The lead LSSL would steam past the landing site, lay down preparatory fire, and take position off the left (upper) flank of the landing area. The accompanying monitors would move above and below the landing area and take position to observe the opposite banks. The armored LCM with embarked units would then execute a right turn when abreast of the landing area, beach and land their troops. The rear LSSL or equivalent would take position off the right (lower) flank of the landing area. Additional forces embarked in other LCMs would maintain station some 1500 meters behind the shock group and move ahead to land on order once the assault units had established a beach head.

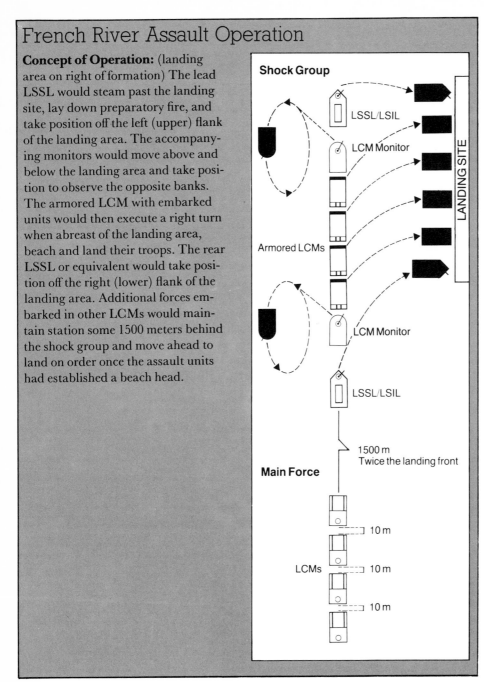

already difficult problem of fire support coordination.

The firefights and landings engaged in by logistic convoys were in the nature of responses to enemy initiatives. The landing units involved were most often of platoon strength (thirty men) and they were ashore only for a short time. Landings of larger forces, such as reinforced infantry battalions, were also undertaken. These were preplanned offensive operations and reflected French initiatives. Such operations were of prolonged duration and required the landing of combat and service support forces as well as quantities of supplies in addition to the assault formations. In their planning and execution these operations most closely resembled the conventional seaborne amphibious assault.

In the case of a preplanned landing, the river convoy formation included a 'shock' group that took position between the opening group and the main body. The shock group, wherein the force commander took station, followed one kilometer behind the opening group. Its purpose was to land the initial assault ele-

ments to secure the landing site and position the fire support craft to facilitate the follow-on landing of the main body. This last remained at some distance, usually just over a kilometer, behind the shock group to allow it the time to complete its initial landing. Once the landing site was secured, the force commander ordered the main body to approach and land. Throughout this operation the fire support boats kept position on the flanks of the landing area while the small craft with the opening group were used to patrol beyond the assembly areas.

The riverine assault landing as described usually worked well. The Viet Minh seldom remained to contest a beachhead. Indeed, the French always sought landing sites that offered the possibility of an unresisted landing on the valid assumption that it was best to deploy the landing force ashore before it became engaged with the enemy. The landings were technically complex, as all landings are, but the more difficult aspect of the riverine operations in Indochina was the maneuver of forces where the terrain severely taxed the infantry and limited the employment of support arms and equipment.

The nature of the river problem is most easily explained in the fact that an assessment of the losses sustained by the French river forces during the Indochina War reveals that these were more serious when the boats were at anchor than when underway. A fixed base by its very nature can be studied by an enemy and, if he is resolute enough and reasonably equipped, he can generally take it when he is ready. The bases used in Indochina varied widely. The simplest were the temporary defenses set up around an anchorage during overnight stops when on operations. On the other end of the scale was the Saigon Arsenal with its drydock and extensive maintenance facilities. The temporary bases and other isolated bases such as those of the coastal forces, had to be self-contained. The larger bases such as Saigon and those of the River Assault Groups long established in the principal river towns, could rely on internal security forces augmented as necessary by outside regional, police or military units. Whatever he circumstances, a river unit commander was never free of the preoc-

Haiphong port facilities included only a floating drydock.

The French Navy arsenal, showing the drydock.

cupation for the security of his base and its essential supplies and facilities.

The Americans adopted mobile afloat bases for their river patrol and assault forces. This provided their river forces with considerable operational autonomy and exploited the defensive capability of large ships. Even so, there always was need for detachments ashore and hence a commitment of resources that had to be drawn from the combat capabilities of the river force as a whole.

The ability of the Viet Minh to attack anchorages varied greatly. In general, temporary anchorages were less vulnerable to enemy action than were the more permanent installations but this was a question of degree. A river force halted for a few hours gave the Viet Minh little time to organize a deliberate attack. Under such conditions the best that he could do was to move in automatic weapons or, preferably, mortars or artillery. When such a threat existed, the French periodically shifted boat anchorages. In places where the waterway allowed, the boats were anchored in midstream in positions from which they could quickly move if fired on.

Where numbers of boats were to be assembled and retained in position for several days, various security arrangements were used. Ground forces, for example, were used to organize perimeter

Incident on the Mekong: Seizure of Thakhek

In the latter part of 1953 the Viet Minh were building roads in the uplands apparently to support operations in Laos. Towards the end of the year, the Viet Minh moved west and entered the town of Thakhek, a French supply point on the Mekong River. Jean Louis Delayen, son of a French Infanterie de Marine officer and already twice wounded, was at that time commanding the North Vietnam Commando Group. This force, engaged primarily in raids along the coast of Tonkin and Annam, had just returned from an operation when Captain Delayen received orders to alert two of his commandos for airlift to Seno, a Laotian airbase near the Mekong River. Upon arrival at Seno, Delayen was told by the general commanding that Thakhek had fallen and a force was being assembled to retake the place. Delayen's mission was to embark his two commandos, reinforced by a heavy weapons unit of the Laotian Army, in whatever boats he could find and proceed upriver as flank guard for the main body that would be marching along the road that paralleled the waterway.

Delayen found an old wood-burning river steamer, the *Francis Garnier*, and several other boats more or less suited to the task and set forth northward as the main body began its movement overland. The boats, however, soon outpaced the ground force that found its progress slowed by obstacles and snipers. Delayen was ordered to reduce speed. However, he had already been forced to allow periodic halts to cut wood for his river boat. He was concerned that continuing at walking pace along the river would allow the Viet Minh to prepare an ambush; indeed, at the last halt he had observed enemy troops although no fire had been exchanged. Acting on his best judgement Delayen continued at speed.

On the third evening, Delayen was within striking distance of Thakhek. Accordingly, he landed his force with the intention of continuing the last few kilometers on foot. As luck would have it, he encountered a Viet Minh truck convoy at a halt.

His commandos promptly dispatched the Viet Minh and loaded on to the trucks. As the column approached the town, Viet Minh sentries allowed it to pass on the assumption that it was the working party returning. Delayen's troops swiftly moved to their pre-assigned objectives and by dawn Thakhek was back in French hands with most of its supplies intact. The general, still some 50 kilometers away, was not too pleased at Delayen's coup since he was accompanied by several press representatives to whom he had promised a front row seat at the recapture of Thakhek. As it turned out, the general was able to stage a second capture of the town for the press and every one was satisfied. Delayen, meanwhile, had quietly left for the coast and his raiding parties where generals were seldom involved.

The venerable wood-burning steamboat Francis Garnier *with part of Delayen's commandos. (ECPA)*

Captain Jean Louis Delayen on his command boat en route to recapture Thakhek, January 1954. (ECPA)

Elements of the two commandos from the North Vietnam Commando Group embarking on a river boat for the move to Thakhek, January 1954. (ECPA)

Heavy Weapons Unit of the Royal Laotian Army assigned as reinforcements to Captain Delayen's commando force. (ECPA)

Delayen, later as a lieutenant colonel.

defenses of the anchorage area. This was costly in men and weapons, however, since both sides of the waterway had to be occupied. Moreover, such deployments complicated the coordination of supporting fire and introduced undesirable delays should the force ashore have to reembark quickly. Another technique, used alone or in addition to the deployment of a force ashore, was to have small boats patrol the periphery of the anchorage and fire on suspicious objects or periodically launch grenades to discourage swimmers. Then, too, boats were protected from floating mines by nets; these were useful but required adjustment to conform to the effect of tides.

The best defense resulted from the ability to mass fires. This required the careful emplacement of weapons ashore and the deliberate positioning of boats to make best use of their armament. In all cases, boats were never allowed to anchor out of range of one another to minimize the possibility of any one boat being attacked and destroyed in isolation.

The preceding discussion has centered on riverine warfare. But, in the reorganization of 1947 when the Naval Brigade was returned to navy command, the River Flotillas became Amphibious Flotillas. These subordinate organizations included river and coastal bases and were clearly intended to serve in both environments. But, the French did relatively little in the way of coastal operations through 1952 beyond engaging in raids with ships' detachments of commandos. The latter were most often used in shore-to-shore operations.

The limiting factor, once again, was that of resources. Coastal operations normally require boat-carrying, sea-going ships to embark the landing force. The French had very few of these and the LSD (landing ship dock) *Foudre*, particularly well suited to the transportation of boats needed for the ship-to-shore movement, did not become available until July 1953. Moreover, most of the landing boats in the area had been modified for service on inland waters and were unsuited for offshore use. Finally, the French troops had little if any amphibious training.

In December 1953 an amphibious training center was established at Cam Ranh Bay where the forces used in the assault phase of Operation 'Atlante' were trained. That operation, conducted at the same time as the siege of Dien Bien Phu, demonstrated the utility of large-scale coastal landing operations. Other such landings were planned but before they could be executed the Indochina War ended.

The French forces sent to Indochina were intended, originally, to join the British and Americans in the war against Japan. It had been planned that they would receive their equipment and training at American facilities, after which they would deploy to the Pacific. The sudden end of World War II nullified these plans and the forces deployed to the Far East without the specialized training that had been anticipated. As a result, amphibious assault operations did not feature prominently in the French strategic thinking in Indochina. It must be admitted that even if greater emphasis had been placed on the value of such operations, the means to execute them were lacking. Associated with this view is the further fact that given the circumstances prevailing in Indochina, the French elected to place their main brown water navy efforts in the deltas which, indeed, were the most important.

PART 3
THE VIETNAM WAR

7
Origins of Vietnamese Naval Forces

The establishment and development of national armies are processes often subjected to foreign influences. This notwithstanding, the armed forces of a country are reflections of the national character and serve as the expression of the national will.

The Vietnamese Armed Forces are largely outside such qualifications. They were created by the French, under whom they were first blooded. They then passed under the tutelage of the Americans, where they received new forms and strengths. But, at no time did they enjoy the measure of independence that made them responsible for their war of national survival. Still, the history of the Vietnamese Armed Forces is largely a reflection of the events that mark the passing of the French, the ascendancy of the Americans, and the ultimate tragedy of the Vietnam War. This transition period will be examined accordingly, first in terms of the naval forces of Vietnam, whose modest scale enables their story to serve as an introduction to the broad panorama of major events that are subsequently addressed.

As 1949 ended, the French had succeeded in creating a government under Bao Dai. But, the initiative was passing to the Viet Minh largely because the French lacked the resources to control an area the size and diversity of Indochina effectively. It was to help compensate for these inadequacies that the French decided to create the Vietnamese Armed Forces.

The Franco-Vietnamese agreement signed in Paris on 30 December 1949 stated that the Vietnamese Armed Forces would include a component whose organization and training was to become the responsibility of the French Navy. In conformance with this agreement, Vice Admiral Ortoli, commanding the naval forces in the Far East, proposed that the Vietnamese Navy begin as a river force. The only other action taken in 1950 was the inclusion of several Vietnamese at the Naval Academy in Brest. None remained beyond the year.

In February 1951 the Ministry in Paris expressed concern that so little had been done. The Admiralty in Saigon replied that all matters relating to the Vietnamese Armed Forces were the concern of the Permanent Military Committee, and that body had yet to meet. Paris insisted that action be taken regardless and, in April, Admiral Ortoli forwarded the first development plan. This proposed to organize two dinassauts under French command and undertake the construction of a recruit training center that year. The center was to be completed in 1952. Then, in 1953, additional river units would be formed. In 1954 auxiliary minesweepers (YMS) would be transferred to Vietnam. Finally, in 1955, an amphibian patrol plane squadron would be organized.

In May the Minister of the Navy advised that he was prepared to accept these proposals with the stipulation that the time schedule be advanced and provision made to include seagoing forces. To this end he announced the intent to transfer a 600-ton 'Chevreuil' type escort to the Vietnamese in 1952, and to begin construction in France of two second class escort ships of the E.50 class (1250 tons) and four minesweepers of the D1 class (365 tons) for the Vietnamese gov-

The commission ceremony of the Cantho Dinassaut, on 10 April 1953, the first unit of the Vietnamese Navy to commission. The Cantho Dinassaut comprising one LCM modified for command missions, two LCMs and two LCVPs armored and armed for riverine operations. (ECPA)

ernment. He also instructed the Admiralty in Saigon to give the highest priority to the development of a budget for the Vietnamese Navy covering the costs of the recruit training center, the recruitment of Vietnamese cadres, and the necessary initial naval construction.

While this activity was taking place in naval circles, the Permanent Military Committee held its first meeting on 1 May 1951. Beginning with this session, it quickly became evident that the Vietnamese government, under the urging of its French advisors and in particular that of General de Lattre, looked to the organization of its armed forces as a single entity, inevitably to be dominated by the army. The navy, disturbed by this attitude, protested to the Minister of the Associated States, stating that it opposed the idea of a navy being nothing more than a service element of the army.

The French Navy was otherwise divided since Admiral Ortoli in Saigon disagreed with Paris over the development plans for the Vietnamese Navy. The admiral insisted that the Vietnamese Navy should begin only with river forces, and that the addition of seagoing units should not be considered at least until

1954. This view eventually prevailed, but the debate continued for some time.

On 15 August 1951 a French naval mission was accredited to the Vietnamese government, and in November the work on the recruit center began. During this same period the French also organized an officer training course aboard one of their gunboats for candidates recruited from among former students of the Hydrography School in Saigon. The Vietnamese Navy was in a fair way to becoming a reality.

Early in 1952 the commander of the French naval forces in the Far East and the high commissioner agreed upon a modified plan for the organizationn of the Vietnamese Navy. This plan provided for the opening of the recruit center at Nhatrang in 1952 as previously proposed. The two naval assault divisions, originally to have been organized in 1951 were to be activated in 1953, when it was also proposed to organize a flotilla of thirty river boats and effect the transfer of one division of three YMSs. The Vietnamese naval staff was to be organized in 1954; in addition, a coastal patrol flotilla was to be formed by integrating the customs service's boats into the navy.

While this proposal was being reviewed, Imperial Ordinance No 2 appeared on 6 March 1952 officially establishing the Navy of Vietnam. Then, on 1 May, the organization of the Vietnamese Armed Forces General Staff entailed a reorganization of the French militiary mission. Incidental to this reorganization on 20 May, a 'Navy Department' was created within the mission charged with 'commanding, administrating, and managing the units of the Vietnamese Navy and directing its development.' In July, Admiral Ortoli presided at the formal opening of the recruit training center at Nhatrang.

One of the most pressing concerns of the navy department within the French mission was to obtain a firm and agreed plan for the development of the Vietnamese Navy. This was becoming ever more difficult as the number of agencies interested in the subject multiplied and the divergent views of Paris and Saigon were not reconciled. To resolve the issue, the Department requested the Franco-Vietnamese High Committee to address the question. But, before the committee could act, the Minister of the Navy in Paris outlined a new long-range program that purportedly reflected the views of the Ministries of Defense and of the Associated States in Paris and of the Admiralty in Saigon. This program provided for the progressive development of the Vietnamese Navy by the organization of units and the acquisition of ships and craft in two phases.

The first phase, beginning in 1953, called for the implementation of the previous Saigon proposal for the organization of two naval assault divisions and one river patrol flotilla of thirty boats, plus the transfer of three YMSs. The year following, two other naval assault divisions were to be formed. The second phase involved the addition of units as follows: 1955 — two minesweepers; 1956 — two coastal patrol ships; 1957 — two coastal patrol ships; 1958 — one minesweeper and one escort ship; 1959 — two coastal patrol ships, one escort ship, and two amphibian patrol plane squadrons.

Armored LCVP of the Vinh Long Dinassaut, the second Vietnamese Navy unit. It was commissioned in June 1953. (ECPA)

As this program was being formulated, the Franco-Vietnamese High Committee met and, at its session of 7 July 1952, agreed that the Vietnamese Navy should be charged with river patrol and coastal surveillance missions. By coincidence, the development plan prepared by the committee in conformity to these missions duplicated the Phase 1 Program announced by the Secretary of the Navy. A plan acceptable to all had finally appeared!

In July 1952, 350 Vietnamese apprentice seamen had been recruited, of whom fifty were to become petty officers. Then, in September, nine Vietnamese Navy officers, representing the first group of locally trained personnel, entered the service. This group was followed by a second class of officer candidates which, like the first, was recruited from among former students at the Hydrography School in Saigon. Additionally, five candidates selected by competitive examination were sent to Brest to enter the Naval Academy there in October.

Progress was being made, but the navy department within the French mission suffered from a shortage of French personnel both to serve as cadres for the Vietnamese Navy and to permit the department to carry out its many duties — not the least of which was to avoid being absorbed by the army. However, the department managed to carry on its work, and as 1952 ended the Vietnamese Navy was a reality; nine Vietnamese officers and 150 men were receiving in-service training aboard various river craft to the French Navy.

The 1952 plans for the development of the Vietnamese Navy, so long in gestation and only recently agreed upon, were once again thrown open to debate in February 1953. That month, the governments of France and Vietnam decided to increase the Vietnamese Army to fifty-seven light infantry battalions to provide added means for offensive operations. Since these operations were to extend into the deltas and along the coastal areas of the country, an increase in the

Vietnamese Navy was also deemed necessary. The matter was referred to the Permanent Military Committee which recomended a supplement to the naval program for 1954 to include the activation of three river flotillas (each composed of LCTs, LCMs, LCVPs, sampans, and river patrol boats), and the addition of one LST and four LSSLs. This augmentation, if adopted, would require the Vietnamese Navy to reach a total strength of 2700 men by the end of the year and the United States to provide military assistance to make up the material shortages.

The supplementary program was forwarded to the Franco-Vietnamese High Committee where it was discussed throughout the remainder of 1953. Incidental to these discussions, the question of whether the army or the navy should control the river flotillas was raised for the first time. It was then that the new commander of French naval forces in the Far East, Vice Admiral Auboyneau, proposed the organization of a Vietnamese Marine Corps.

Armored LCM. The workhorse of the Vietnamese River Force was the armored LCM6. This boat carried a crew of seven and was armed with three 20 mm cannon and two .50 caliber machine-guns. It served both as a troop carrier and as a logistic support boat for the French and the Vietnamese. It carried 120 troops or 32 tons of cargo. (USN)

French commandement, a modified LCM 6 used for command in riverine assault operations. Note the high seat to enable an observer to see over river banks.

On 10 April 1953 the first unit of the Vietnamese Navy, still with French cadres but under its own flag, was activated. This was the *Cantho* Dinassaut comprising one LCM (command), two LCMs and two LCVPs. At the end of the same month, the French assigned LSIL *9033*, under French flag, to the training center at Nhatrang. Later, in June, the *Vinh Long* Dinassaut was activated. These activations and assignments raised the 'flag' question, and debate over this issue became sufficiently lengthy and acrimonious to suspend all transfers of ships and craft, other than river craft, to the Vietnamese for the remainder of 1953. Among the French, some wanted Vietnamese ships to fly a 'tricolor' jack, others wanted the Vietnamese commission pennant to include the national colors of both countries, and still others wanted to devise a completely new flag for the French Union. The Vietnamese simply held that their ships should fly Vietnamese national flags and commission pennants.

While these arguments waxed and waned, the navy department of the French mission decided that it would be prudent to recruit the added Vietnamese needed to bring the navy up to the strength of 2700 men. The Franco-Vietnamese High Committee had not yet agreed to the supplementary naval program for 1954 — nor would it ever — but the Navy Department considered that the training of additional Vietnamese was fully warranted, particularly since enlisted specialists were henceforth to be trained at Nhatrang, where the charter of the recruit training center had recently been expanded.

As 1953 drew to its close, it was painfully evident that the Vietnamese Navy had progressed very little in the course of four years. The upset early in the year in what had momentarily appeared as a firm development plan had not been resolved, nor were there any central guidelines to follow. The French Navy staff and the Vietnamese Armed Forces General Staff each had its separate program, and the Vietnamese Navy appeared destined to continue to live a hand-to-mouth existence. A further handicap of the Vietnamese Navy was the joining of all of the Vietnamese military services under a single general staff and single budget in June 1953. This was most serious for the infant Vietnamese Navy, for its strength of only two dinassauts, corresponding to about .5 per cent. of the strength of the Vietnamese Armed Forces, made it appear so inconsequential that it was

largely ignored by the Vietnamese government. As a result, the fortunes of the Vietnamese Navy depended upon actions taken at subordinate echelons — actions which tended to be influenced far more by local events than by any long-range plans. There was, therefore, an urgent need to convince the government that even a small navy could not be organized without a reasonable plan that extended several years into the future and provided the basis for orderly procurement, construction, recruitment, and training of personnel.

The Franco-Vietnamese High Committee eventually acknowledged this need, and at its session of 15 February 1954 adopted the concept of a five-year naval development plan. The committee also considered that personnel of the navy should be designated as fleet personnel to man sea-going ships, large river craft, and service units, and as marine corps personnel to man river patrol craft and dinassauts and to form commandos and a one-battalion landing force. The committee further recommended a substantial development program that by 1958 would have provided the Vietnamese Navy with four dinassauts, nine minesweepers, six escort ships (two of 600 tons and four of 2000), four LSMs, four LSSLs, seven LCT/LCUs, sixteen coastal patrol boats, eight river gunboats (250-ton), five coast patrol ships, and one hydrographic survey ship. This program was concurred in by all agencies concerned and was forwarded to the Vietnamese and French governments in March 1954 for approval.

Shortly before, on 11 February 1954, the flag issue having been resolved, the French transferred three YMSs to the Vietnamese. This was followed in March by the transfer of two LCUs and Dinassaut *22*, and in August by the transfer of Dinassaut *25*. By the time the Indochina War ended in July of that year, the Vietnamese Navy consisted of four naval assault divisions, three YMSs, two LCUs, the naval schools at Nhatrang, and two receiving stations — one in Saigon and the other in Haiphong. The personnel strengths also increased. In January 1954 the Vietnamese Navy mustered twenty-two officers and 684 men; by July this had grown to forty-five

Saigon Navy Yard anchorage with LSSL HQ 230 *and LST* HQ 502 *(ex-U.S.S.* Cayuga County*).*

Left
LSIL HQ 331 *and LSSL* HQ 228 *in Saigon Navy Yard drydock.*

Opposite
South Vietnam Navy Ninh Giang, *ex-U.S. Navy LSM 85, displaced 1095 tons, made 12 knots and was armed with four 20 mm and two 40 mm cannons.* (VNN)

officers and 975 men. On 30 October 1954 the Vietnamese Navy had 131 officers and midshipmen, and 1353 enlisted men. Of these, eighty-six midshipmen and 233 enlisted men were in schools in Vietnam and France.

With the end of hostilities and the withdrawal of the French from Tonkin, the Vietnamese General Staff considered that the five-year plan submitted in March by the Franco-Vietnamese High Committee had to be modified. Accordingly, Major General Nguyen Van Hinh, Chief of the General Staff, recommended on 27 October that, by the end of 1954, the Vietnamese Navy include a shore establishment comprising a naval headquarters and a receiving station in Saigon; the naval schools at Nhatrang; river bases at Mytho, Cantho, Vinh Long, Faifoo (Hoi An), Tam Ky, and Quang Ngai; boat repair facilities at Hue, Mytho, and Cantho; and marine corps facilities necessary to the corps' growth. The operating forces were to include four dinassauts, two escort ships of 600 tons, two coastal patrol ships, two LSMs, three YMSs, two LSSLs, four LCUs, sixteen coastal patrol boats, and three LCUs repair craft. The marine

The French commandant of the Vietnamese Navy Training Center at Nhatrang receives Lieutenant Generals John W. O'Daniel USA (left) and Samuel T. Williams USA (right), the outgoing and incoming Chiefs U.S. MAAG.

Left
He receives Captain Jean Recher FN (left) and Lieutenant Commander Le Quang My VNN (center), the outgoing and incoming commanders of the Vietnamese Navy.

corps was a consist of a headquarters, four river companies for duty with the dinassauts, and a one-battalion landing force.

General Hinh further recommended that in 1955 the shore establishment be expanded and improved as necessary to include a naval communications facility, and that three coastal patrol ships, three AMSs, two LSMs and one hydrographic survey ship be added to the navy. He also proposed the addition of three commando and six light support companies to the marine corps. To meet these programs, he anticipated that personnel strength at the end of 1955 would reach 160 officers and 3300 men in the navy and ninety officers and 3730 men in the marine corps. The French cadres required for such a force were listed as sixty officers and 370 petty officers of the navy and twenty officers and 165 NCOs of the colonial army.

The marine corps appeared in these proposals because there had been a number of specialized formations among the Vietnamese units that had been organized by the French during the war which, although in the army, were intended to serve with the river and inshore coastal forces of the navy. This association had been found to be particularly important in the case of river forces, and all such units routinely operated with an infantry element attached. The inventory of these special army units included a 420-man amphibious battalion equipped with thirty-seven M29C 'weasels' and thirteen LVT(4)s.

The regularization of these relationships, an issue of discussion since the preceding year, was achieved on 13 October 1954 when a government decree signed by Ngo Dinh Diem set forth articles as follows:

Article 1. Effective 1 October 1954 there is created within the Naval Establishment a corps of infantry specializing in the surveillance of waterways and amphibious operations on coasts and rivers to be designated THE MARINE CORPS.

Article 3. The Marine Corps shall consist of various type units suited to their functions and either already existing in the army or naval forces or to be created in accordance with the development plan for the armed forces.

Article 4. These units will be of the following types; River Companies, Landing Battalions, Light Support Companies, Commandos, and Naval Assault Divisions.

The proposal, endorsed by General Hinh and collaborated in by the French, was destined like all its predecessors to be overtaken by events. It also marked the last time that the future of the Vietnamese Navy would be discussed solely between the French and the Vietnamese. Thenceforth, United States officers would enter into the deliberations. Eventually, Americans would replace the French in advisory functions but just when and under what circumstances remained unclear, since General Hinh had indicated French cadres would be present in numbers in the Vietnamese Navy to the end of 1955.

At the time of the 1954 Geneva Agreements the United States had 342 military personnel serving in the Military Assistance and Advisory Group (MAAG) Indochina. This group, whose strength was not to be exceeded by virtue of the Agreement, had been primarily concerned with 'assistance' to the French in the nature of equipment and supplies. Its 'advisory' function had related only to the utilization of American equipment and had had nothing to do with operations or training. These last domains had been and remained entirely the province of the French. Indeed, Chief MAAG had obtained agreement to the assignment of American liaison officers to the French Commander-in-Chief's headquarters in Saigon only in early 1954 but none had yet been assigned when the war was ended.

In the final stage of the war the French Expeditionary Corps in Indochina totalled 230,000 men, of whom 105,000 were Indochinese serving in either regular or auxiliary units. In addition, there were 226,000 men in the armed forces of the Associated States. The vast majority of the Asian contingents in all cases were Vietnamese. Thus, when the Indochina War ended, there were some 300,000 Vietnamese under arms. Further, while the French were withdrawing forces from Vietnam in a process that was accelerated when the Algerian rebellion broke out in November 1954, it was evident the

French intended to retain a presence in the country. This, the new Commander of French Naval Forces Far East, Vice Admiral Jozan, had explained, was to enable France to meet its obligations under the Manila Pact, signed in September.

Ngo Dinh Diem did not encourage these French views. On the contrary, he pressed for the complete and early withdrawal of the French Expeditionary Corps. This was to have a major impact upon the Vietnamese Armed Forces for they had been receiving their support from the French, who were using resources provided by the United States. With the cessation of hostilities, U.S. military assistance to the French in Indochina ceased, and title to material previously provided reverted to the U.S. The United States then undertook the direct support of the Vietnamese military establishment.

In late 1954 the United States had announced its readiness to support the Vietnamese Armed Forces at a level of 90,000 men. This position had been opposed by Saigon and in early 1955 the figure was revised to 100,000 men. Then, later in the year, the figure was raised to 150,000 where it remained until the expansion of the U.S. effort in 1961.

United States involvement in the support of the Vietnamese Armed Forces inevitably entailed matters of organization and training that previously had been exclusive French responsibilities. As an initial step toward providing the necessary coordination, officers of the U.S. MAAG and of the French Mission were brought together in late 1954 into an Advisory, Training and Operations Mission (ATOM).

On 15 January 1955 the U.S. Navy member of the Senior Team, ATOM, proposed missions for the Vietnamese Navy and Marine Corps that included limited amphibious operations, river and coastal patrol, minesweeping, fire support, and logistic support for military forces. However, the force levels in ships and craft recommended were below those required for such missions; this was little more than a valiant effort to fit the Vietnamese Naval Forces into the 3000-man ceiling imposed under the overall Vietnamese Armed Forces strength of 100,000 set by the United States at that time.

In November 1955 Lieutenant General John W. O'Daniel, Chief of the U.S. Military Assistance and Advisory Group in Saigon makes a farewell call on President Ngo Dinh Diem accompanied by Lt. Col. Croizat.

Shortly after this proposal appeared, an agreement was reached with the French wherein Lieutenant General O'Daniel, Chief MAAG Vietnam, would assume responsibility for the organization and training of the Vietnamese Armed Forces under the overall authority of the French High Commissioner. At that time ATOM was reorganized and redesignated as the Training, Relations and Instructions Mission (TRIM). The new organization consisted of 225 French and 120 U.S. personnel. The Navy Division of TRIM, initially composed of three U.S. and two French officers, was headed by a French Navy captain who also commanded the Vietnamese Navy and was the senior navy officer in the French mission. Under the circumstances, the advisory function of the U.S. officers was scarcely onerous.

The Navy Division TRIM nevertheless prepared a new plan for the development of the Vietnamese naval forces, which was approved and forwarded by the Chief of TRIM to the Minister of Defense on 28 April 1955. This plan, like its ATOM predecessor, was concerned primarily with fitting forces into the 3000 man ceiling. The force levels thus continued unrealistic in terms of the missions contemplated and did little more than reveal that since the end of the war the French had transferred to the Vietnamese Navy one LSSL, two LSILs, and two LCUs to add to the three YMSs and two LCUs on hand at the end of hostilities. Further, the plan envisaged, in the case of the Vietnamese Marine Corps, a crippling cut to 1000 from the 2373-man strength that existed, on 31 December 1954. This, admittedly, was in part compensated for by charging the amphibious battalion of 700 men intended for service with the navy to the army ceiling. This, however, could not be accepted as a permanent arrangement.

As these events were unfolding, the

Captain Harry Day USN (on right), Chief of the Navy Section of the U.S. Military Assistance and Advisory Group, Indochina in 1955.

Vietnamese were becoming increasingly anxious to assume full control over their armed forces. The date which the French and Americans had agreed would allow time for the organization and staffing of the headquarters and service elements needed by the Vietnamese naval establishment to operate on its own, 30 June 1956, became too remote for the Vietnamese.

As a first measure, a headquarters for the Vietnamese Marine Corps was established on 1 May 1955. This made it possible to focus the American inspired effort to bring together the varied units of the marine corps into a two-battalion force with the ultimate view of progressing on to a regiment. Then, Chief TRIM announced that the Vietnamese Navy would become independent on 31 December 1955, but on 30 June 1955 Premier Diem assigned the Deputy Chief of Staff of the Vietnamese Armed Forces additional duties as the Naval Deputy on the General Staff. This made Army Brigadier General Tran Van Don the head

of the Vietnamese Navy. The arragement was short-lived; on 20 August the Premier appointed Lieutenant Commander Le Quang My as the Naval Deputy and Commander of the Vietnamese Navy. Commander My promptly replaced all French personnel in command assignments in the Vietnamese naval forces with Vietnamese. The French retained command only of the naval schools, but this too was terminated on 7 November 1955. When this rapid sequence of events ended, the French found themselves with nothing more than the advisory functions comparable to those of American personnel; the French released from command assignments moved to TRIM.

This development, harmonizing functions between American and French personnel, came at the time when the ceiling for the Vietnamese Armed Forces was raised to 150,000. This brought the authorized strength of the Vietnamese naval forces to 4000, of which 1837 were to be marines. As a consequence of these events and the accelerated reduction of

French naval forces in Vietnam, the expanded Navy Division at TRIM, in collaboration with Vietnamese officers, undertook a detailed review of the overall Vietnamese naval establishment. This, together with a survey of French naval resources in-country that could be transferred to the Vietnamese, provided the basis for two organization and development plans for the Vietnamese naval forces.

The first of these was a reorganization plan intended to utilize only available resources and provide an immediate capability to continue some of the coastal and inland waterways patrol tasks being surrendered by the French. The plan would also give to the navy the essentials of the command, administrative, and logistic systems needed for it to gain a measure of

RPC of RAG 27. These 11-meter River Patrol craft had twin diesels which gave them a speed of 15 knots. They were intended for patrolling but could carry fourteen men plus the crew of three. RPC's had one twin .50 caliber and two .30 caliber machine-guns.

autonomy. Additionally, it was envisaged that the navy should have the means of furnishing limited water transport for the army and further provide an amphibious force able to take its place alongside the army's parachute regiment as the country's general military reserve.

The reorganization plan corresponding to the foregoing considerations required a navy of 2845 men organized into three components. The shore establishment was to include a naval headquarters and service elements; four coastal commands with headquarters at Saigon, Nhatrang, Qhuinhon, and Danang; the naval schools at Nhatrang; four river force bases at Cantho, Mytho, Long Xuyen, and Vinh Long; and three boat repair facilities at Saigon, Cantho, and Danang. The second component, the Sea Force, was to consist of five patrol craft (PC), three auxiliary mine sweepers (YMS), two landing ship support, large (LSSL), two landing ship medium (LSM), and ten coast guard patrol cutters. The third component, the River Force, was to include five dinassauts, each with six LCM, four LCVP, and five outboard motor boats; four landing ship infantry large (LSIL); five landing craft utility (LCU); and four harbor craft (YTL). The Vietnamese Marine Corps, totalling 1835 men, was to be formed into a two-battalion force with appropriate headquarters.

The planned strength of 4680 was 680 over the authorized ceiling. Moreover, the five PCs intended for the Sea Force represented an increase of three ships above then current force levels. These augmentations were considered modest in terms of the expanded responsibilities being assumed by the Vietnamese naval forces and were allowed to go forward by Chief TRIM to the Chief of Staff of the Vietnamese Armed Forces on 1 November 1955.

On 7 December 1955, Lieutenant General Le Van Ty convened a conference at his headquarters to discuss naval matters. He first approved the reorganization plan. This authorized the increase in ceiling for the naval forces and the consolidation of the diverse units of the marine corps into the two-battalion force proposed; the details of the marine corps organization were to be published on 21 December by Commander My.

General Ty then turned the discussion to the future of the naval forces. The TRIM officers present thereupon tabled a two-year development plan that had been prepared on the assumption that the reorganization plan would be approved. The development plan called for an expansion of the naval forces to 9000 men by 1957 to provide a Coastal Patrol Force and a River Force which, with the necessary shore facilities, could assume responsibility for the denial of inland and coastal waters to illegal traffic. In addition, the lift capacity was to be raised to enable the conduct of amphibious opera-

Patrol motor gunboat, the HQ 610 Ding Hai. A 95-ton patrol ship able to make 16 knots, it was armed with one 40 mm and two 20 mm cannons and two machine-guns.

Lieutenant General Le Van Ty, Chief of Staff of the Vietnamese Armed Forces, Saigon 7 March 1956.

tions at the regimental level. The marine corps was to be increased to a three-battalion regiment and the force formally recognized as part of the country's general reserve. Finally, the necessary headquarters and shore facilities required to support the operating forces were to be expanded or established.

The development plan concluded that to carry out the missions contemplated the minimum forces required by the end of 1957 for the Coastal Patrol Force were four destroyer escorts (DE), ten PC and twenty-seven motor patrol boats (CGUB). The River Force would need five dinassauts, each with nine LCM and eight LCVP; four LSIL, two LSSL, and four LCU; the Transport Force would include four LST and four LSM. Finally, one squadron of amphibian patrol planes would be activated.

Following discussion of the development plan, General Ty expressed his agreement with it in principle and added that he would accept a compensatory reduction in army strengths if this became necessary to remain within authorized force ceilings. The future of the Vietnamese naval forces, at long last, appeared assured.

The jointly prepared development plans marked the final French contribution to the process that brought the Vietnamese naval forces into being. From the first the French had stressed the importance of river forces and, indeed, had conceived the naval assault division organization that had proven itself so effective. The French also had observed the importance of infantry elements with river forces and had organized specialized ground force elements to serve with the afloat formations. This last provided the basis for what became the Vietnamese Marine Corps. Further, the French anticipated the need for the Vietnamese to have a coastal patrol force and looked to its eventual creation along with a patrol plane squadron. Finally, the French insistence on the early establishment of the naval schools at Nhatrang as the first step in the development of a navy was most pertinent.

The legacy of the French to the Vietnamese Navy was substantial. Its organizational structure was essentially French but, after 1956, the impact of American operational procedures and practices became dominant. The Vietnamese Marine Corps, in contrast, was a creation of the United States. The French had recognized the need for specially trained ground combat units to be integrated with the river forces and to provide an amphibious assault capability, but they had approached the requirement by the creation of different units for each of the tasks. The United States approach was that a marine corps made up of uniformly trained and centrally administered men could better provide task organizations tailored to specific missions while retaining its identity and basic combat capabilities. This was the concept under which the Vietnamese Marine Corps came to be established.

8
The Post Geneva Decade

The Vietnamese Armed Forces established at the mid-point of the Indochina War remained operational throughout the post-Geneva transition period and played a major rôle in the Vietnam War that followed. The naval component, a mere 4000 out of an American supported strength of 150,000 was equally active and wielded an influence well beyond its numbers. This was evident in the navy, which served as the medium through which the French riverine warfare experience reached the Americans. It was also notable in the marine corps which formed, with the army's parachute regiment, the country's general reserve and, as such, was used in many combat operations from the start. Their role notwithstanding, the Vietnamese naval forces were but a small part of a large cast engaged in an agonizing drama. The interrelationship of circumstances that determined this drama is better seen from a broader perspective.

In the earlier narrative on the French experience, reference was made to the differences that often existed on matters of government policy and the conduct of military operations between Paris and Saigon and among the senior authorities in Indochina. This situation did not alter materially after the Americans became the dominant influence in the region.

When in 1954 the question was asked whether or not military support should be provided to South Vietnam, the U.S. Joint Chiefs of Staff revealed themselves opposed, whereas the Secretary of State believed support necessary. Its nature and extent, however, were contingent on several factors. First, the signing of the Manila Pact on 8 September 1954 had provided South Vietnam with a protective umbrella. This protection was conditional but its very existence was a clear sign that the eight signatory powers recognized the importance of the country to the security of the region. One could be-

lieve that South Vietnam would not be allowed to fall without a fight.

As the communists continued to gain in power, western governments had become increasingly interested in the establishment of some system of collective security in the Pacific area. Some time before the Geneva Accords were concluded, several governments were considering a Southeast Asia defense pact.

The headquarters of the Southeast Asia Treaty Organization in Bangkok, Thailand in 1962. The headquarters was eventually shifted to new facilities, by which time the effectiveness of the organization had waned considerably.

SEATO officers prepare to depart on an area reconnaissance in up-country Thailand in late 1962. SEATO had a regular program of field visits whose dual objective was to ascertain the conditions of the main roads and waterways of the country and provide an area orientation to officers who might have to conduct operations in the treaty area.

Following upon these deliberations a conference was held in Manila where the Southeast Asia Collective Defense Treaty was signed on 8 September 1954. The key to the Manila Pact signed by the United States, the United Kingdom, France, Pakistan, Australia, New Zealand, the Philippines and Thailand is Article IV which affirmed that each party recognized that an attack on any one

of them would endanger the peace and security of all. Article VIII defined the treaty area as Southeast Asia and the southwest Pacific. A protocol extended the benefits of defense protection and economic cooperation to Cambodia, Laos and the Republic of Vietnam.

The Treaty Organization (SEATO) established in Bangkok was headed by a Secretary General who received his guidance from the SEATO Council. The Council met annually. The Council Representatives, comprising the ambassadors of the member nations in Bangkok, provided the continuity of action. SEATO headquarters also included a Military Planning Office which received its direction from the Military Advisors. These met at the time of the Council and once again in the intervening period. The Military Advisors Representatives at SEATO headquarters were responsible for ensuring that the plans developed by the MPO were consistent with national capabilities and conformed to national guidance.

The Special Assistant to the Secretary General was charged with the Office of Counter-Subversion and each year met with national representatives to review and update the intelligence estimate upon which the Military Planning Office based its contingency plans. The Military Planning Office was also involved in preparation of SEATO military exercises. In the years between 1955 and 1962 there were 23 such exercises, one of which, Tulungan, involved 78 ships, 400 aircraft and 37,000 troops.

Another consideration was the presence of the French Expeditionary Corps. As long as it remained in Vietnam, it would discourage the North Vietnamese from any overt move towards the South. This, in turn would provide the time needed for the Americans to restructure the Vietnamese Armed Forces into a balanced military establishment able to assume operational responsibilities well beyond their then current capabilities.

The Vietnamese Army established by the French in 1950 had been limited to units not exceeding battalion strength. The later creation of a Vietnamese general staff still left a wide gap between the top command and its tactical field units. There was also an absence of logistic

Post-Geneva Operations *The Geneva Accords of mid-1954 brought only an uneasy peace to Vietnam. While some communist troops did leave the south for return to the north, sufficient numbers remained behind to keep the infection active. These staybehind elements were concentrated in the Plain of Reeds and Ca Mau areas of the Mekong delta and in several coastal areas of Annam that had never been cleared. As a result, the Vietnamese Navy made every effort to maintain a presence on the major waterways even as it was trying to absorb additional ships, boats, equipment and personnel.*

LSSL on patrol in the lower Mekong delta area in 1955.

Vietnamese dinassaut on patrol in Mekong delta waterway in 1955.

Vietnamese LCVP on patrol: note crew members opening footbridge to allow boat to pass.

Commander James Ross, USN, one of the first American advisors to the Vietnam Navy, aboard on LCVP on patrol in the lower Mekong delta area in 1955. Note: while U.S. advisors were not allowed to accompany Vietnamese units into combat at that time, nothing prohibited participation in patrol operations.

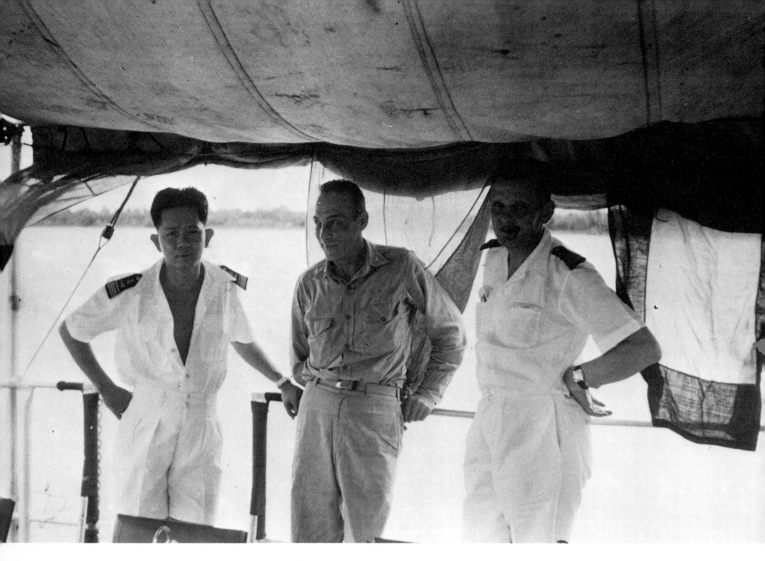

Captain Jean Recher, French Navy, last French officer to command the Vietnamese Navy, with Commander Ross and Commander Le Quang My, the first commander of the Vietnamese Navy, aboard an LSSL during 1955 visit to dinassaut bases on the lower Mekong River.

organization because this responsibility had remained French. If the Vietnamese military establishment was to become autonomous, the Americans would have to build up a supporting foundation as well as reorganize the tactical forces into larger units. This would take time and the French were in the best position to provide it. In these circumstances the initial task envisaged for the Vietnamese Armed Forces was internal security, with a limited capability to resist an attack from North Vietnam. This, the United States believed could be accomplished with a 90,000-man army.

The French, like the Americans, were confronted by opposing sentiments. After the Geneva Agreement the French were quite prepared to leave Indochina. The

troubles in Algeria were making this all the more desirable. At the same time, the obligations the French had accepted under the Manila Pact could best be met by their continuing presence in Southeast Asia. The French also had economic interests in the region that should not be abandoned. The Americans' interest in seeing the Expeditionary Corps remain was counterbalanced by their impatience over the dominant influence of the French throughout the South Vietnamese military establishment. Until the French left, the Americans argued that they would be denied the freedom of action they thought necessary for them to develop the Vietnamese forces. The Vietnamese, for their part, were simply anxious for the French to go and the then Premier Ngo Dinh Diem was doing all he could to hasten their departure.

Retired General J. Lawton Collins, sent to Saigon by President Eisenhower an interim ambassador, reached an agreement with French General Ely on 13 December 1954, wherein the French

Opposite above
SEATO officers visit the headquarters of U.S. forces in Thailand in May 1962. Officers from left to right include Colonel Akbar, Pakistan; Major General John Wilton, Chief of the Military Planning Office and later Chief of the Australian Joint Staff; Captain Garnett, United Kingdom; Lieutenant General Richardson, USA, commander U.S. forces in Thailand; Colonel Purcell, New Zealand; Colonel Croizat, U.S.A. Colonel Britsch, France; Colonel Castillo, Philippines; Colonel Abichart, Thailand; Captain Savage, Australia.

Opposite
In May 1964 Vice Admiral Thomas Moorer, USN, commander of the U.S. Seventh Fleet visited SEATO headquarters in Bangkok. He was received by Secretary General Konthi (Thailand), Deputy Secretary General Worth (Australia) and Colonel Croizat (U.S. Military Advisors Representative).

agreed to share the training responsibility for the South Vietnamese forces beginning on 1 January 1955. The order and pace of the events that followed was soon changed when the French began to withdraw their Expeditionary Corps on the premise that the United States was not providing the level of support anticipated. This decision, which was to bring an end to the French presence in Indochina in April 1956, may also have been influenced by Diem's replacement of the pro-French Chief of the Vietnamese General Staff, General Nguyen Van Hinh, with a more tractable individual.

Whatever the reason, the decision of the French to withdraw their forces caused General Collins to revise his plans for a six-division South Vietnamese Army to accept an increase in the forces to be supported to a new level of 150,000; this was to be in addition to the Civil Guard and Village Self Defense Forces already agreed upon.

Inherent in these developments were several problems. The first was the disagreement among the Americans as to the type of training to be provided to the paramilitary forces. The U.S. military in Saigon wanted the Civil Guard, as the province's chief area security force, to have military training and be administered within the Ministry of Defence. The U.S. Embassy argued for police-type training and inclusion within the Ministry of the Interior. The latter view prevailed, but by 1959 the ineffectiveness of the Civil Guard had been clearly demonstrated and the decision was reversed.

Another problem was that of the organization of the army. The plan for the six-division force to back up the French had had to be changed. To meet its expanded responsibilities it was now planned to form four field divisions and ten (later seven) light divisions. In addition, there would be thirteen regiments for service as territorial forces. This organization, even with the increase in force levels, was less than the numbers of Vietnamese in uniform when the Indochina War ended. Hence, the reorganization of the military involved a partial demobilization. It was also painfully apparent that the 342 Americans making up the MAAG Vietnam were alone incapable of

taking on the task of reorganizing and training the Vietnamese Armed Forces. An augmentation of this group was not possible under terms of the Geneva Agreement, which the United States respected even though it had not been a signatory. A request to double the number of Americans, nonetheless, had been forwarded to India, which chaired the International Control Commission. A reply was being awaited.

In the midst of these troublesome issues, the Binh Xuyen and the religious sects, whose security forces had been supported by the French, levied demands on Premier Diem to continue such support, which he could not accept. In the spring of 1955 the situation had become serious. On 21 March the Hoa Hao went into dissidence. The Binh Xuyen then began to rebel but, being near the capital, their headquarters was destroyed on 28 March and Diem was able to impose a truce three days later. At the same time, the Cao Dai decided to accept Diem's offer to integrate part of their forces into the army. Diem then turned his attention to the Hoa Hao, but before that problem could be settled the Binh Xuyen returned to the fray, this time in Saigon proper. Diem, who by then had the army fighting the Hoa Hao, also turned his troops against the Binh Xuyen. By mid-May they had been crushed, and shortly thereafter the back of the Hoa Hao rebellion was broken.

It is said that the Vietnamese soul is the product of three influences, Buddhism, Taoism, and Confucionism. Whether or not that is so, the Vietnamese are evidently susceptible to varied ideologies, some with qualities readily adapted to political ends. Thus it was that Catholicism could gain the allegiance of certain villages and two provinces in the north, and that the Cao Dai would come to claim more than one million adherents. The French made use of the sects by supporting their self defense forces and freeing themselves of this onerous responsibility. The Catholic militias were actually created by the French and served under military command. The Cao Dai and Hoa Hao, however, had their own armies. These sects pledged their allegiance to the French but retained command of their

forces even when these were supported by the French. The Binh Xuyen in contrast, had no religious affiliation and essentially represented a pirate band turned legitimate.

Of these groups, other than the Catholics, the Cao Dai were the largest and most formally structured. The Cao Dai movement, whose patron saints include Victor Hugo and Sun Yat Sen, began in Cochinchina in 1926. While strongly religious in aspiration, its leaders have always looked for a strong voice in politics. The Hoa Hao movement, an offshoot of Buddhism, was born of revelations that came to Huynh Phu So in 1939 in the course of a strange illness. The sect had its center in the Mekong delta area adjoining Cambodia. Like the Cao Dai, the Hoa Hao leaders were not unaware of the political power that control of military forces provided. The Binh Xuyen began as a group loyal to the Viet Minh, but, when driven out of the Rung Sat where they had made their base, they offered their services to the French.

It is evident that the loyalties of the Cao Dai, Hoa Hao and Binh Xuyen were directed inwards. Thus, the story of their relations with the French and other Vietnamese groups is not one of mutual trust and harmony. The Binh Xuyen, in particular, made the mistake of revolting against the Saigon government in April 1955.

The victory of the government forces against the sects greatly strengthened the position of Diem. The efforts of Emperor Bao Dai who, with French urging, was seeking to remove Diem were thenceforth futile; these ended in any event on 26 October when the Republic of Vietnam was proclaimed with Ngo Dinh Diem as its president. The creditable performance of the army also enhanced its image and gave it a needed confidence. Unfortunately, the commitment of army and marine corps units against the sects also delayed their planned reorganization. This problem continued when the national forces were ordered to take over large areas formerly under Viet Minh control. The first such operation, south of the Mekong River delta near Camau, was difficult because the population was particularly hostile. However, the deployment of two regiments into a com-

Traditional Buddhist temple in Tonkin countryside.

Below left
Catholic paramilitary militia, North Vietnam 1954.

Cao Dai temple at Tay Ninh.

Interior of Cao Dai Temple at Tay Ninh.

The fighting between the National Army and the dissident Vietnamese Binh Xuyen in April 1955 did extensive damage to the native area lying between the communities of Saigon and Cholon.

munist area in central Annam went off very well.

Despite the delay in the reorganization of the armed forces, the Franco-American training mission, TRIM, was able to continue some training and, most important, work toward creating the logistic organization the Vietnamese lacked. The principal difficulty in all these activities was the shortage of experienced Vietnamese officers and an effective higher headquarters. Still, as 1955 progressed there were signs of increasing tranquility in the countryside. Then, in 1956, the MAAG was augmented by 350 new arrivals. Finally, on 28 April the French High Command was disestablished and with it TRIM; advisory responsibilities thereafter were wholly American.

President Diem earlier had announced his opposition to the elections aimed at reunifying the country called for by the Geneva Agreement. The Hanoi government had registered its distress over this decision but neither the Chinese nor the Russians appeared ready to force the issue. Still, the threat of overt communist action remained very real. Because of this, the MAAG decided to recommend the deployment of the army to block invasion routes from the north and west and also cover the Mekong River delta. This would provide for an initial defense against overt aggression and concurrently contribute to the internal security by having forces in the main population centers. This dispersal of ground forces would also lessen their vulnerability in the event of a surprise attack.

In this same period, the navy's Sea Force, operating in five coastal zones, was working to maintain a coastal patrol with little success. Its attempt to better the situation by creating a paramilitary organization of fishermen with junks to provide an inshore patrol capability was not approved, however. The fortunes of the River Force were little better. The five River Assault Groups (RAGs), each able to embark an infantry battalion, were infrequently used for assault operations. Rather, the army under whose command the RAGs were serving, preferred to use the boats for logistic missions which, as often happened, were no less hazardous.

Above
Premier Diem accompanied by his brother the Archbishop Ngo Dinh Thuc and General Le Van Ty, Chief of the General Staff (back to camera) await start of ceremony.

Below
The Premier's party varied with his visits. On the occasion shown he was accompanied by four senior staff generals. The second from the right is General Tran Van Don who was a member of the triumvirate that overthrew Diem in 1963.

Two Vietnam River Force patrol boats (STCAN/
FOM) on routine reconnaissance mission, on South
Vietnam inland waterways, 1966. (USN)

The Yabuta was a Japanese-designed motor junk
which became the principal junk in the Coastal Force.

The date set for the elections passed without incident. President Diem then undertook a number of actions that were to have undesirable consequences. First, he abolished the system of elected village officials in favor of appointees. Then, he reduced support for several civic action programs that had gained popular interest. Further, he encouraged a denunciation campaign which resulted in several thousand individuals of unproven convictions being sent to political re-education camps. The reaction of the people to these actions was notably unfavorable. This was all the more unfortunate because the Hanoi government had decided, when the elections were not held, to return communist cadres to the South to revitalize militant elements that had stayed behind. This renewed effort to subvert the South fell on freshly-prepared, fertile ground.

In 1957 communist insurgency turned vicious, with the start of a reign of terror against local village officials. Neither the Civil Guard nor the Village Self Defense Force were able to contain the spread of this violence, and the military became increasingly involved in countering the insurgency. Still, the Vietnamese Army retained as its primary rôle defense against overt aggression and, on 1 November, the I Corps became operational in the northern part of South Vietnam. This was followed in April 1958 by the establishment of II Corps with its headquarters in Pleiku, to the west. At that time, a provisional III Corps headquarters was created in Saigon.

President Diem had attributed the growing insurgency to last ditch efforts by communist stay-behind forces. The use of the military against such elements was not believed necessary on a continuing basis. But, by 1959, the communist attacks were being directed at the security forces, and these actions could no longer be seen as rearguard operations. The army was then called upon to commit company-size intervention forces. The communists riposted by operating in battalion strength and the army's intervention companies had to be increased correspondingly. The navy also increased its commitments by finally creating the Junk Force first proposed in 1956.

Despite these developments, the situation did not improve materially in 1960. Indeed, in November of that same year a number of officers launched an abortive coup against Diem. The next month, the communists formed the National Front for the Liberation of South Vietnam and the drive was on to force the South to join the North in a reunited, communist Vietnam.

The MAAG had been following this evolution closely and had anticipated the need for intensifying its activities. To that end, in late 1960, the MAAG had completed a counter-insurgency plan which recommended the increase of the Vietnamese Armed Forces to a ceiling of 170,000 and the Civil Guard to a strength of 68,000 men. President Kennedy accepted these recommendations on 28 January 1961. Soon thereafter the principal mission of the Vietnamese Armed Forces was changed from counter-invasion to counter-insurgency.

The strengthened MAAG still was not able to have advisors assigned below army regimental level. Further, the effectiveness of the advisors was limited be-

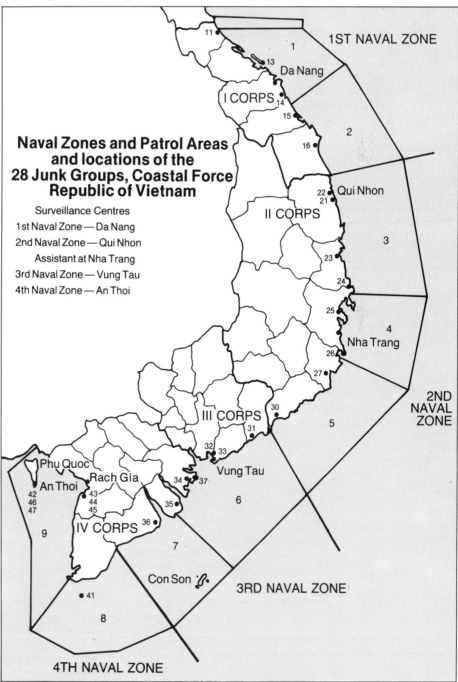

Commandement. Modified LCM used as a command boat for riverine assault operations. This 20 meter boat had a speed of 8 knots and was armed with two 20 mm cannons, two .30 and two .50 caliber machine-guns and one 81 mm mortar in a well behind the forward turret. (USN)

cause they were not permitted to accompany their Vietnamese units into combat. The small increase of the MAAG to 795 in number authorized in April 1961 was of some help. More important was the precedent set by the U.S. Marines who later that year obtained permission to have their advisors accompany the Vietnamese Marine Corps units in combat as 'observers'. In this same midyear period, the U.S. Marines instituted a program of on-the-job training wherein selected junior ranks were sent to Vietnam for a two-week combat orientation; this program was suspended in 1962 but reinstated in 1963.

The year 1961 continued as one of increasing American involvement. Late in the year, U.S. Navy minesweepers added a new dimension to American operations when they joined South Vietnam Navy forces in a barrier patrol south of the 17th parallel. More important was the fact-finding mission of U.S. Army General Maxwell D. Taylor, who called for more

active American participation in Vietnam in the form of a 'limited partnership'. He also recommended the deployment of three U.S. Army helicopter companies and six to eight thousand troops for base defense purposes. Then in December, President Kennedy further augmented the numbers of American advisors in South Vietnam and authorized them to accompany Vietnamese units in combat.

The year 1961 also marked the shift from the Agroville to the Strategic Hamlet Program. The Agroville Program of 1959 was intended to resettle rural families in government-built communities where they would enjoy improved social and economic advantages. The latter did not materialize and the Viet Cong, as the southern communist irregulars were now

*Opposite above and right
Monitor. Modified LCM armed with one 40 mm cannon, two 20 mm cannons, one .50 caliber machine-gun and one 81 mm mortar. This 18 meter boat was capable of 8 knots and had a crew of ten. (USN)*

Vietnamese Brown Water Operation

Vietnamese River Assault Group 22 was assigned a resupply mission along the Saigon River from 5 to 7 July 1965. The force comprised three monitors, seven LCM, two LCVP, eight patrol boats (FOM), eight Civil Guard LCVP and two civilian motor barges. The move was to be supported by U.S. Army observation aircraft, artillery in position and helicopters available on call. A supplementary task to evacuate a Vietnamese Army unit and some civilians out of Ben Suc was added after the force moved out the evening of 5 July. After a halt to pick up additional cargo the force resumed movement at 0215 on 6 July. At 0800, the lead monitor was mined but suffered little damage. Helicopters were called in to strafe ahead of the force as it continued its movement. At 1430, the force arrived at its destination and unloaded the supplies. It got underway for Ben Suc at 1600 and arrived at 1800, after attracting sniper fire most of the way. At Ben Suc the personnel to be evacuated were loaded and the force moved out at 1830. At 1910, a mine was detonated near an LCM with no damage; at 1925, another exploded near a monitor again with no damage. Then, at 2110, LCM *1054*, loaded with civilians, was mined and began receiving heavy fire. Artillery fire was called in on enemy positions while several patrol boats and LCVPs picked up survivors. The unengaged boats beached away from the enemy position. Incidental to these moves a patrol boat was mined and LCM *1528* received several rocket hits. At 2340, orders were received for the force to return to Ben Suc where it arrived at 0145 on the morning of 7 July without further incident. Subsequent efforts to salvage LCM *1504*

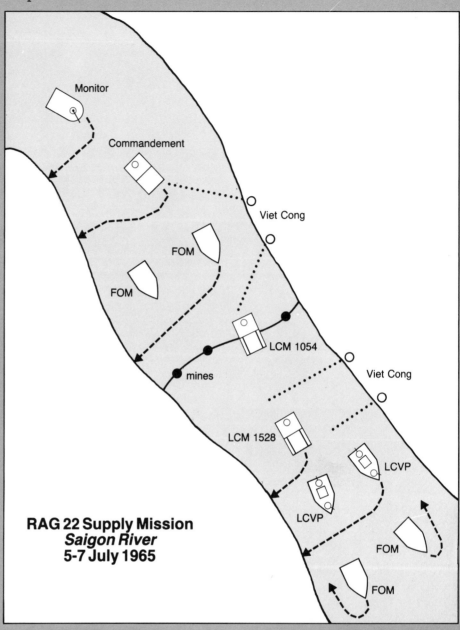

RAG 22 Supply Mission
Saigon River
5-7 July 1965

were unsuccessful and the boat was destroyed by explosives. The operation resulted in thirty-five Vietnamese military and civilian personnel killed. It is startling to record that the force included two patrol boats equipped

with mine detecting sonars which no one knew how to operate. Moreover, of the two LCVPs in the force which were equipped with minesweeping drags only one was operating the equipment.

Opposite
The South Vietnam Navy Sea Force Chi Lang *II, ex-USS* Gayety, *MSF 239, was transferred in 1962 for use as escort and patrol ship. The Navy Sea Force operated seven Patrol Craft in 1965.* (USN)

labelled, soon found the agrovilles lucrative targets. To lessen their vulnerability, the agrovilles were fortified and the Strategic Hamlet Program was born.

The idea of this new but related program was to select areas that would first be cleared of Viet Cong. Then, a fortified community would be built wherein the people could assure their own defense. The goal of this effort, which like its predecessor was inspired by the British experience in the Malayan Emergency, was to create 11,000 strategic hamlets. These would accommodate and shelter the bulk of the rural population and frustrate Viet Cong efforts to subvert the people. Unfortunately, the merits of the concept were not tested and the program was implemented with unwarranted haste. Its effectiveness proved marginal and the question of the value of this costly program and its applicability to the South Vietnam environment remains unsettled.

The year 1962 was one of ever increasing commitments. Already at the end of 1961 the Americans had begun to deploy military units, as differentiated from military advisors. Two U.S. Army helicopter companies had been sent to South Vietnam and the U.S. Air Force had moved in a composite detachment for training and attack missions. The deployment of other similar U.S. Army and Air Force units continued in 1962; then, in April, the U.S. Marine Corps brought a large helicopter force to Soc Trang in the lower delta area of the III Corps area. All these American units, which soon totalled 3000 men, were intended solely to support the field operations of the Vietnamese Armed Forces and not to engage in independent actions. Moreover, their personnel rotated after only a short time 'in-country'; as an example, when the U.S. Marines shifted their helicopter force to the north to support I Corps, the tour of their personnel was extended from four to six months.

These developments were paralleled by organizational changes that confirmed the intensification of the struggle. On the South Vietnamese side, the Mekong River delta was separated from III Corps and formed into a new IV Corps. On the American side, the MAAG was subordinated to a newly created U.S. Military Assistance Command, Vietnam (USMACV). Lastly, the communists in the south formed the Central Office for South Vietnam (COSVN) to coordinate Viet Cong military actions with political activities more effectively.

The Vietnamese Marine Corps

The King and Queen of Thailand receive General Paul Harkins USA, first commander of the U.S. Military Assistance Command, Vietnam and Lieutenant General James Richardson, USA, commander of U.S. forces in Thailand in June 1962.

reached brigade strength in 1962. As part of the general reserve, its units had been repeatedly engaged in combat operations where they had gained an excellent reputation. This was maintained throughout the year during the execution of twelve amphibious operations and eight helicopter assaults. Then, the Corps ushered in 1963 with a brigade-level amphibious landing on the communist-infested Camau peninsula south of the delta. Still, as 1963 progressed, the situation in the South steadily worsened. The strategic hamlet and pacification efforts were failing and confusion and uncertainty prevailed in the Saigon government. Meanwhile, the communist enemy gained strength with each passing day.

In November 1963 President Diem was overthrown and killed. Three weeks later President Kennedy was assassinated. As the shock waves of these events dissipated, American plans to withdraw some forces from Vietnam were set aside. President Johnson, newly sworn in, was convinced that holding South Vietnam was politically desirable. Secretary of Defense McNamara, an equally impatient man, was distrustful of neutralism and argued for further increases in the support being given to the South Vietnamese.

The extension of the American involvement in South Vietnam in 1964 did not materially improve the situation. In January, the Saigon government underwent another coup. In March, Secretary McNamara visited Saigon and came away convinced that the regime was ineffective. He called for general mobilization for South Vietnam and the preparation of a plan to bomb North Vietnam. In this same period, the Regional Forces became the Civil Guard and the Village Self Defense Forces were redesignated Popular Forces. In other administrative changes, General Westmoreland replaced General Harkins in June as Commander, U.S. Military Assistance Command, Vietnam (COMUSMAV) and the MAAG organization within MACV was disbanded.

Then, in August, occurred the famous Gulf of Tonkin incident wherein U.S. Navy ships in international waters were attacked by North Vietnamese naval units. The American reply was an air strike again North Vietnam followed on 6 August 1964 by President Johnson receiving from the Congress of the United States the authority to engage U.S. forces in combat in South Vietnam. This escalation moved ahead, despite a report made by a Canadian envoy recently returned from Hanoi informing Washington that the government of North Vietnam would not bow to threats or the use of force.

The importance of the Mekong delta

Vietnamese Brown Water Action

HQ *226* of the Vietnam Navy Sea Force was assigned river patrol duties in the delta area in September-October 1965. The U.S. advisor's report reveals that it provided protection for three salvage operations seeking to recover RAG boats and engaged in nine fire support and two logistic missions and thirteen independent patrols. He assessed its performance as 'outstanding' in particular, citing an action when it was escorting RAG 23 with the 41st Vietnamese Ranger Battalion embarked. This action took place on the Ham Luong River in Kien Hoa Province on 4–5 October; 21 Vietnamese rangers and sailors were killed and 57 were wounded. The operation began at 0700 at Ben Tre with the embarkation of the rangers who were to land downriver and seek out a VC unit that had earlier attacked friendly outposts and villages. A previous attempt to airlift the rangers into the VC area had been cancelled because of adverse weather. The river force got underway at 1100 escorted by a U.S. Army observation plane which reported no enemy activity. At 1200 the LSSL in the lead fired on a suspected enemy position (XS 515209). Immediately heavy enemy fire was received by RAG boats from the right bank and the LSSL from the left. Two LCMs were hit; one in sinking condition was taken in tow by the other, both beaching on the left shore where the survivors landed and set up a perimeter defense. All other RAG boats withdrew but the LSSL remained on station to maintain supporting fire. Air strikes were called in. The boats returned landing more troops to reinforce the perimeter. The LSSL and RAG units stayed on hand during the night to cover the troops ashore. Next day, search operations cleared the area of VC. Next morning, the 6th, a salvage unit took in tow the heavily damaged LCM. Reembarking the remaining troops, the force returned to Ben Tre that afternoon.

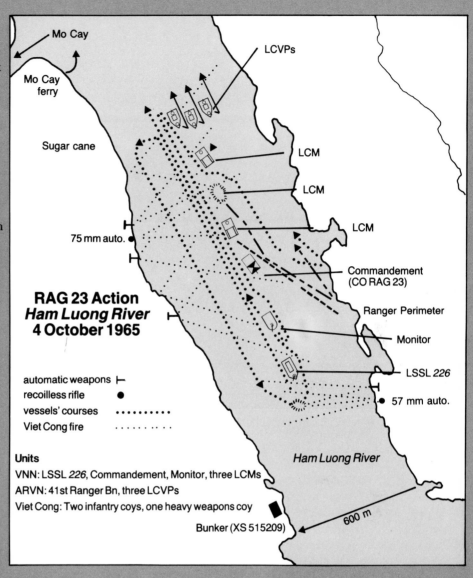

RAG 23 Action
Ham Luong River
4 October 1965

automatic weapons ⊢
recoilless rifle ●
vessels' courses ∙∙∙∙∙∙∙∙∙∙
Viet Cong fire ∙ ∙ ∙ ∙ ∙ ∙ ∙ ∙

Units
VNN: LSSL *226*, Commandement, Monitor, three LCMs
ARVN: 41st Ranger Bn, three LCVPs
Viet Cong: Two infantry coys, one heavy weapons coy

Bunker (XS 515209)
600 m

HQ 226, Linh Kiem *of the Vietnamese Navy Sea Force assigned to river patrol duty during the period 16 September to 18 October 1965 when it engaged in the Ham Luong River action. This LSSL was originally LSSL 9022 of the U.S. Navy and was transferred to France in 1951 for service during the Indochina War as the* Arquebuse. *It was acquired by the Vietnamese in 1955. (VNN)*

area had always been well appreciated by the Vietnamese. By 1964, when American involvement intensified greatly, the Vietnamese Navy's River Force had been built up to seven River Assault Groups each with nineteen boats, one River Transport Escort Group with thirty boats, and one River Transport Group of seven LCUs. These were located at six bases and served under the operational control of the Vietnamese Army. This force already compared very favorably to the six dinassauts that the French had organized for service in the whole of Indochina.

In addition, the Vietnamese Army itself had five boat platoons, two in III Corps area and three in IV Corps. Each of these platoons had fifty of the 5-meter plastic assault boats equipped with a 45-horsepower outboard motor. The River Assault Groups had no infantry attached and were primarily used for logistic and occasional combat operations rather than for routine patrolling. The army's assault boats were available for short patrols but were mainly used for crossing waterways. Military patrolling, as such, was most limited.

Beyond the military units, there were paramilitary forces in the delta also equipped with boats. The regional forces had twenty-four boat companies and a total of 169 LCP-type boats. Civilian irregular defense groups had 150 of the 5-meter plastic assault boats. Additionally, the customs service, which put men aboard all international ships moving up-river to Cambodia, had 1700 men at fifty-one locations in the delta and operated twenty-three patrol boats.

The national police had perhaps the most ambitious program of all. This arose from the assignment given by the Government to the Director of National Police on 26 October 1964 to undertake 'resources control'. The American economic aid mission, under whose aegis the advisors to the national police functioned, immediately launched a survey of the delta area to determine how best this tremendous task could be accompanied.

The Resources Control Plan that resulted called for an increase of 12,000 men to man 649 check-points, of which 306 were to be located on or adjacent to the principal waterways. Posts concerned with waterborne traffic were to be equipped with 466 of the 5-meter plastic assault boats for intercept duties. In addition, eleven locations were to be organized as bases for river control units to be equipped with a total of seventy-six LCP-type boats and 152 plastic assault boats. These were intended to operate in pairs, two LCP towing two plastic boats to a mid-channel position to form a floating checkpoint. This same organization was to be used at night to maintain station at known enemy crossing points to intercept illegal traffic. Finally, the American advisors anticipated that the national police would request the navy 'to assist in preventing Viet Cong movement by coastal routes, preventing entry into the delta area of reinforcements and supplies, and, lastly, to transport personnel for operations and support their efforts in the major channels of the river.'

In January 1965 MACV had evidence of the presence of North Vietnamese forces in South Vietnam. In response to this presence and a series of other hostile actions, the Americans launched 'Flaming Dart', the code name for reprisal air attacks against North Vietnam that began on 2 March; 'Flaming Dart' eventually became 'Rolling Thunder', the sustained American air campaign against the North. At the time that the United States began its air strikes in support of operations in the South and against targets in the North, a 30-meter long steel ship was seized along the coast of South Vietnam carrying arms and munitions to the Viet Cong. This incident attracted attention to the coastal patrol capabilities of South Vietnam's navy and raised the question of involving the U.S. Navy in the task. Then, on 7 March 1965 the 9th U.S. Marine Corps Expeditionary Brigade landed over the beaches near Danang.

Shortly after the landing of the marines, the U.S. Navy established a force under the code name 'Market Time' to conduct coastal surveillance and anti-infiltration operations. 'Market Time' forces included nine U.S. Navy radar picket ships and minesweepers and seven patrol aircraft for offshore surveillance. An inshore patrol force was also organized. This consisted of 15-meter Swift boats (PCF) and 25-meter U.S. Coast Guard patrol boats (WPB). The Swift boats operated in the seven inner costal areas while the larger coast guard boats ran the barrier patrols in the two coastal areas adjacent to the 17th parallel and Cambodia. All U.S. operations were coordinated with those of the South Vietnamese Navy Sea Force and Coastal Force. The latter was the old Junk Force, which had lost its para military status and been integrated into the navy under new designation.

Thus, by mid-1965 the United States had engaged its land, sea, and air forces in combat operations in South Vietnam. Escalation thereafter was rapid. By August there were 125,000 American combat troops in South Vietnam; two years later the number had quadrupled. The Vietnam War was well and truly on.

South Vietnam Navy, Ships and Craft, 1955–1965

The Vietnamese Navy was created by the French. But, by the end of the Indochina War it remained primarily a modest river navy and had only the beginnings of a sea-going capability. It underwent an initial expansion with the transfer from the French, upon their departure, of ships and craft, the French had originally received from the Americans. Thereafter the Vietnamese Navy was equipped and trained by Americans. Until 1965, the Vietnamese Navy operated its ships and craft with support of the United States. Then, in that year, the United States deployed its own combat forces into Vietnam and these brought with them improved models of inshore coastal and river patrol boats and of riverine assault boats. Several years of combined and coordinated brown water naval operations followed.

South Vietnam Navy Sea Force

In 1965, the Vietnamese Navy's Sea Force had some 2000 personnel manning 45 ships. These were responsible for coastal patrol; three to four of the seven patrol craft (CP/PCF/MSF), twelve patrol motor gunboats (PGM) and

Above
The South Vietnam Navy's Kim Qui, *ex-U.S. Navy PGM 605, powered by twin diesel engines, had a maximum speed of 17 knots. Armament consisted of one 40 mm, two 20 mm cannons and two .50 caliber machine-guns. (VNN).*

Below
Vietnamese Navy Sea Force Patrol Vessel HQ05 Tay Ket. This ship launched in September 1943 as the USS PC 1143 was transferred to the French where it served in Indochina as the Glaive *prior to being turned over to the Vietnamese in 1956. This 450-ton ship is normally armed with one 3-in gun, one 40 mm cannon and four 20 mm cannons. (VNN)*

three coastal minesweepers (MSC) were normally kept on station in each of the four Naval Zones. The operation of these ships was coordinated with those of the U.S. Navy's Task Force 115 ('Market Time') through the Coastal Surveillance Centers.

The second operational mission of the Sea Force was patrol of inland waterways and support of River Assault Group operations. Two of the five LSSLs and five LSILs were maintained in the major Mekong waterways for this purpose. In addition, another one of these ships was available to the Commander, Rung Sat Special Zone for patrol of that difficult area on the approach to Saigon. The Sea Force also had twelve 50-foot motor launch minesweepers used to sweep moored mines and magnetic and acoustic bottom mines. These boats could also sweep shore-controlled river mines but for River Assault Group operations that task was normally carried out by RAG boats equipped with grapnels.

The third mission of the Sea Force was supply. This was given over to the three LSTs and seven LSMs on an as-required basis. Of note is that one of the LSMs was equipped as a hospital ship with modular surgery, X-ray, dental, laboratory and treatment room trailers mounted on the well deck.

HQ 226. This 42-meter LSSL (landing ship support, large) of 385 tons could do 15 knots. It could carry 60 troops. However, the French and Vietnamese used these LSSLs and LSILs for command and fire support in riverine assault and escort operations. The 3-inch gun plus three twin 40 mm guns and four single 20 mm guns made the LSSL a formidable fire support base.

South Vietnam Navy coastal minesweeper Bach Dang, ex-U.S. Navy MSC 283, displaced 270 tons, made 13 knots and was armed with two 20 mm cannons. (VNN)

HQ 327. This 48.6-meter LSIL (landing ship infantry, large) of 393 tons could do 12 knots. It could carry 12 tons of cargo and 76 troops but was used by the French and Vietnamese as a command and fire support ship on the rivers.

Above
HQ 226 and HQ 405. The latter is an LSM (landing ship, medium) of 63 meters and 1095 tons. Capable of 13 knots, an LSM could lift 250 tons or 400 troops.

Below
South Vietnam Navy LST Camranh, ex-U.S. Navy USS Marion County LST 975, displaced 4080 tons, made 11 knots and was armed with eight 40 mm cannons. (VNN)

South Vietnam Navy Coastal Force

When the Vietnamese Navy took on the task of patrolling the coast in 1956, it soon realized that it had neither the personnel nor the material resources to perform satisfactorily. Accordingly, it proposed to the U.S. mission in Saigon the organization of a force of junks to conduct inshore patrols in sensitive areas. The idea was that junks manned by locally recruited civilians, trained by the navy and working in coordination with the national police could easily mingle with local boat traffic to observe and report on maritime activity in designated key locations. This proposal was eventually adopted in 1960 and by 1961 there were 80 sailing junks operating off the coast of the I Corps area below the 17th parallel.

In 1962 the U.S. mission proposed an expansion of the Junk Force to include 84 command junks, 100 motor-sail junks, 140 motor junks and 320 sail junks. Plans were also made to established five coastal repair facilities and assign responsibility for the defense of force bases to the Regional Forces. These plans were implemented in 1963. Then, in 1964, when the relative ineffectiveness of the sail junk had been demonstrated, the U.S.-Japanese designed Yabuta was introduced as a replacement.

At the time the Americans organized their coastal surveillance for 'Market Time', the Junk Force was integrated into the Vietnamese Navy as the Coastal Force. When on 1 July 1965 this new designation became effective, the Coastal Force numbered 4000 personnel and had 389 motor junks and 95 sail junks organized into 28 groups based at 22 locations (see map). While the force was to grow to include over 600 junks, it remained plagued by shortages of personnel and supplies. The Vietnamese Navy supply organization was centered in Saigon and was ill-equipped to support an organization as widely dispersed as the Coastal Force. This dispersion, moreover, made the bases particularly vulnerable to Viet Cong attack. The problem of base defense was yet another difficulty that was never satisfactorily resolved.

Typical coastal groups of the 1965–66 period operating in the north generally consisted of three command junks, three motor-sail junks and sixteen sail junks (gradually replaced by the Yabutas). In the south the typical group had three command and six motor-sail junks. This organization varied from group to group and changed as additional boats entered the inventory. Such variations were also found in the various types of junks used. These, other than for the Yabutas, were locally manufactured and varied accordingly. In general, the five types of junks used by the Vietnamese Navy Coastal Force had characteristics as follows:

Command Junk length 17 m, beam 5 m; armament: one each .30 and .50 caliber machine-guns, plus crew weapons. *Motor-Sail Junk* length 13 m, beam 3.7 m; armament: crew weapons only. *Motor Junk* length 11.5 m, beam 2.6 m; armament: crew weapons only. *Sail Junk* length 9.7 m, beam 2 m; armament: crew weapons only. *Yabuta Junk* length 16.9 m, beam 3.4 m; armament: one each .30 and .50 machine-guns and one 60 mm mortar, plus crew weapons.

Above
South Vietnam command junk of Coastal Group 37. These craft used for inshore patrols mounted one .50 and one .30 caliber machine-guns and a 60 mm mortar amidships. (USN)

Opposite right
A Yabuta fitting out after being launched in Saigon shipyard.

Opposite left
Sail only junk, the main type.

Left
Motor-sail junk of the Vietnamese Navy Coastal Force. These boats were similar to but slightly larger than the older sailing junks. Both categories were unarmed. The only weapons available were those of the individual crew members. (VNN)

Above
Motor only junk of the Vietnamese Navy Coastal Force. These wooden boats were unarmed. The only weapons at hand were those of the individual crew members. (VNN)

South Vietnam Navy River Force

Vietnamese served with French naval forces and in commandos assigned to the dinassauts during the Indochina War. In addition, provisions were made for the organization of a Vietnamese Navy as part of the Vietnamese Armed Forces. Because the French authorities in Saigon considered that Vietnam should begin with a river navy while Paris headquarters preferred a more elaborate start, nothing was done for two years. Then, on 10 April 1953, when the Saigon view had prevailed, the Cantho Dinassaut was established as the first naval unit under Vietnamese colors. This unit comprised one command LCM, two armored LCMs and two armored LCVPs. In June 1953, the similarly equipped Vinh Long Dinassaut was added, followed by two more dinassauts activated in 1954 just before the end of the Indochina War.

When, after the Geneva Accords, the Americans joined the French in the initial reorganization and training of the Vietnamese Armed Forces, a recommendation was made to, and approved by, the Chief of the Vietnamese General Staff on 7 December 1955 to increase the river forces to five dinassauts each equipped with six armored LCMs, four armored LCVPs and six outboard motor boats. On the same day, the Chief of the Vietnamese General Staff, General Le Van Ty, also approved a development plan calling for increasing the dinassaut allowance to nine LCMs and eight LCVPs.

By 1965 the name dinassaut had passed into history. The River Force of the Vietnamese Navy then comprised seven River Assault Groups (RAGs). Six of these were equipped with one commandement, one monitor, five armored LCMs, six armored LCVPs and six patrol boats (STCAN/FOM) each. The seventh, RAG 27, had one commandement, one monitor, six armored LCMs and ten river patrol craft (RPC).

In addition, the River Force also included one River Transport Escort Group (RTEG) and a River Transport Group (RTG). The former had four monitors, six patrol boats (STCAN/FOM), and twenty armored LCVPs; the latter was equipped with seven LCUs (landing craft utility).

Commandement. Modified LCM used as a command boat for riverine assault operations. This 20 meter boat had a speed of 8 knots and was armed with two 20 mm cannons, two .30 and two .50 caliber machine-guns and one 81 mm mortar in a well behind the forward 20 mm gun. The new model shown had revolving gun turrets, a radar and better accommodations for its 10 man crew. (USN)

An armored troop carrier, originally an LCM 6.

These two groups were based in Saigon. The tactical groups were deployed two at Mytho and one each at Nha Be, Vinh Long, Cantho, Long Xuyen and Saigon.

The RAGs, each with 150 Vietnamese personnel and three U.S. advisors, were tasked with embarking, transporting and providing fire support for riverine assault forces. They were also used for logistic support, patrol escort and minesweeping missions. The RTEG, with 180 Vietnamese personnel, was specifically intended to escort rice and charcoal convoys from the delta area to Saigon markets. The RTG, with 60 Vietnamese, served as the major transport force on the rivers. Of particular note is that RAG 22 based at Nha Be, near Saigon, was assigned to the Rung Sat Special Zone. That area, on the approaches to the port of Saigon, was a Vietnamese Navy command directly subordinated to the Commander of the Navy and included six Regional Force companies, nine Popular Force platoons, one Regional Forces boat company and the aforementioned RAG.

Armored LCVP: The companion boat to the LCM was the smaller landing craft, vehicle and personnel widely used in the Pacific War before being armored and fitted with one 20 mm cannon and three .30 caliber machine-guns for the Indochina river war. It carried 36 troops or 3.5 tons of cargo. (USN)

Patrol Boat (STCAN/FOM). This 11 meter French designed boat was extensively used during the Indochina War. Its 'V' shaped hull made it resistant to mine explosions and it was consequently used to sweep mines. It was relatively slow, 10 knots, but was armored and carried one .50 and three .30 caliber machine-guns with a crew of eight. STCAN stands for Services Techniques des Constructions et Armes Navales and refers to the French government agency charged with naval construction: FOM stands for France Outre Mer and refers to items built overseas. (USN)

A further item of note is that the reorganization plan approved in December 1955 included four LSILs in the River Force. The two-year development plan approved on the same day envisaged the addition of two LSSLs. As it happened, these ships and others like them that were later transferred to the Vietnamese never became part of the River Force but were retained in the Sea Force. Nonetheless, the LSSL and LSIL were used regularly to patrol the major inland waterways and in support of River Assault Group operations.

Rung Sat Special Zone (RSSZ)

The difficult Rung Sat area, a vast, dense mangrove swamp between Saigon and the sea used by the communists as a transit zone between III and IV Corps Areas and for supply depots and other facilities, was declared a 'Special Zone' in 1964 and assigned to the Vietnamese Navy as its only territorial command. The Commander, Rung Sat Special Zone was given the mission to deny the area to the communists. For this purpose, he had under his command six Regional Force

companies totalling 600 men, nine Popular Force platoons totalling 270 men, one Regional boat company of forty men, and eight LCVPs, plus the services of one RAG and, as mentioned, one Navy Sea Force LSSL or LSIL was available for patrol and support. In 1966, most of the Mekong Delta was in the IV Corps Tactical Zone but Gia Dinh and Long An Provinces and the RSSZ in the north (see maps on pages 95 and 134) were part of the III Corps Tactical Zone. The U.S. MRF conducted operations and training in the RSSZ.

The monitor. This modified LCM carried one 40 mm and two 20 mm cannons, one .50 caliber machine-gun and one 81 mm mortar. It was also armored.

River patrol craft (RPC) used by River Assault Group 27 of the Vietnam Navy at Mthyo. Capable of 14 knots, the RPC mounted two twin .50 caliber and one single .30 caliber machine-guns. (USN)

Land Craft, Utility (LCU). These 180 ton American built boats had three diesels and three shafts giving a speed of 10 knots and very good maneuverability. They displaced 360 tons under full load and were armed with two 20 mm. cannon. All seven of these craft were in the River Transport Group of the Vietnam Navy River Force. (USN)

9
The American Brown Water Navy

The struggle for Indochina that occupied more than a third of a century varied widely in scope, intensity, and sponsorship. Its first phase began in 1940 with the arrival of the Japanese. This phase continued without too great turmoil until the spring of 1945, when it exploded into violence a few months before coming to an abrupt end. The French phase, that of the Indochina War, followed. This second phase contributed to the consolidation of communist power and brought an end to the French presence on the peninsula in 1954. The third phase involved ten years of American assistance and advisory support to the South Vietnamese. This was accompanied by increasing frustrations and worsening conditions until it culminated in 1965 with the commitment of U.S. military forces in the area. The fourth phase encompassed a second ten-year period wherein American combat power was rapidly built up, vigorously applied, and then progressively transferred to the South Vietnamese. The final phase ended in 1975 with the collapse of the South Vietnamese Armed Forces that followed after the withdrawal of the last American units.

The American decision to engage forces in Vietnam was not made in ignorance of the costly logistic implications. These had been studied at the time of the Indochina War and their magnitude had helped discourage direct American involvement in support of the French. This attitude no longer prevailed in 1965 and the energetic General Westmoreland enjoyed ready access to America's resources. These were used with lavish hand to build ports and airfields and to provide vast quantities of arms and equipment of all types. The measure of what all that entailed is beyond human dimension. That the bomb tonnages dropped on Indochinese targets well exceeded those of World War II adds little

to an understanding of the magnitude of the effort. More finite perhaps are the five thousand military aircraft lost between 1960 and 1969, from the time that U.S. air support operations began to when they reached their peak. It was in this frontier-like atmosphere where all seemed possible and nothing appeared beyond reach that the American brown water navy came into being.

In the initial organization of the Vietnamese Armed Forces, the French had given priority to creating a river navy. When the Indochina War ended, the River Force was an operating entity. The new Sea Force, however, suddenly faced with the responsibility for the patrol of the long coast of South Vietnam, was not up to the task. The U.S. Navy's first concern was to remedy that situation.

Despite intensified training and the creation of the paramilitary Junk Force, the Vietnamese Navy's coastal patrol capabilities remained marginal. Accordingly, in late 1961, ocean-going American minesweepers began to patrol the waters near the 17th parallel. This effort was extended into the Gulf of Thailand off the Cambodian border in early 1962. The American units were not authorized to intercept Vietnamese ships but they used their radars to vector Vietnamese Sea Force units to investigate suspicious contacts. Still, even with the improved effectiveness of the coastal patrol operation, there was little evidence of significant infiltration activity.

The situation changed in 1964 when the North Vietnamese began to supply weapons to the Viet Cong on a large scale. In early 1965, following the pre-

U.S. Coast Guard cutter Point Glover *operating out of Phu Quoc Island (1965). At 1250 hours on 19 September 1965, the* Point Glover *sank a six-meter motor junk later found to have six contraband weapons and 480 rounds of ammunition. At 2330 the same day another coast guard WPB, the* Point Marone, *returned fire and sank a twelve-meter motor junk. Both actions took place off Ha Tien near the border of Cambodia. (USN)*

viously mentioned 'Vung Ro Incident' when a North Vietnamese steel-hulled ship loaded with arms was intercepted and driven ashore, it became apparent that supplies for the Viet Cong were moving by sea as well as land. It was further noted that seaborne infiltration was carried on by junks moving close inshore where they could mingle with local traffic and by larger sea-going ships sailing on international waters except for their brief runs to offloading sites on the coast. This pattern of communist maritime activity suggested that the Vietnamese Sea Force and Junk Force should intensify their efforts to intercept illicit inshore traffic while the U.S Navy took on the offshore surveillance task.

The concept of such a combined operation was proposed by General Westmoreland and was approved by the U.S. Joint Chiefs of Staff on 16 March 1965. On that same day, Task Force 71 of the Seventh Fleet assumed responsibility for what, on 24 March, became known as 'Market Time'. Although this was an air and sea effort, most of the action was carried on by surface units which, on 11 May, were authorized to stop, search, and seize vessels within and beyond South Vietnam's territorial waters.

Operational control of 'Market Time' passed from the Seventh Fleet to the Commander, Coastal Surveillance Force (Task Force 115) on 30 July 1965. This, thenceforth, placed the effort directly under COMUSMACV, but operations remained unchanged. These were conducted in four coastal zones, corresponding roughly to seaward extensions of the four corps areas. The four coastal zones, in turn, were divided into nine patrol areas. Each area, extending seaward up to 60 kilometers, was patrolled by a U.S. Navy oceangoing minesweeper, radar picket ship or, later, by 50-meter high speed patrol gunboats (PG). Inshore patrols were conducted by the U.S. Navy's Swifts and larger U.S. Coast Guard boats. A continuous air patrol was also maintained over the whole of the coastal defense area.

This array of American ships, aircraft and boats backed by the Seventh Fleet was intended to supplement the efforts of the Vietnamese Sea Force and Coastal Force until such time when they could assume responsibility for the whole of the effort themselves.

In 1966 the Sea Force, with sixty American advisors, was maintaining sixteen ships at sea. The Coastal Force with its twenty-eight groups and over 600 junks had 135 American advisors and maintained as many as 190 junks on inshore patrol at any one time. Coordination of the combined operation was effected through five Coastal Surveillance Centers located at Danang, Quinhon, Nhatrang, Vung Tau, and Anthoi (Phu Quoc Island), each with parallel American and Vietnamese communications channels to their respective headquarters in Saigon.

To strengthen further the security of the country's ports, five Harbor Entrance Control Posts were organized later. These HECPs, operating under the code name 'Stable Door', maintained 24-hour radar and visual surveillance over harbor approaches and anchorages. They also had harbor craft available to intercept and search suspicious boats and objects. In the aggregate, 'Market Time', the Vietnamese Navy's coastal operations, and 'Stable Door' achieved positive results, but the work was tedious and, for the Americans, often frustrating.

A sampling of American Sea Force advisors' reports reveals the nature of the average patrol mission. The advisor's log of the month-long patrol of a Sea Force ship in September 1965 reveals that 169 junks and 902 persons were searched. It also reports that the Vietnamese ship suffered a radar and reefer failure, neither of which could be repaired because the maintenance personnel required had been sent off on shore leave. Lastly, there are several entries reporting that the ship just 'cruised' and the American advisor was unable to convince the Vietnamese ship commander he should patrol sea areas regularly used by coastal traffic, rather than wide stretches of empty sea. The report of another advisor on a later patrol repeats the same story; 152 junks and 741 persons searched, shipboard radar failure that could not be repaired, tedious cruising in aimless fashion, and a lack of initiative on the part of the Vietnamese commander.

Despite such difficulties, 'Market Time', 'Stable Door', and their Viet-namese adjuncts made seaborne infiltration a hazardous adventure. Already in 1966 tightened coastal patrols were credited with having forced the communists to change their supply methods. At the beginning of that year, it was estimated that as much as three quarters of the Viet Cong's supplies were coming in by water. By the end of the year, this had been reduced to 10 per cent of the total. By 1967 operations resulted in 10,000 suspects intercepted and interrogated and several tons of contraband captured. A year later, coastal forces were boarding and searching some half a million junks annually. Moreover, it was noted that in the first three years of operation, 'Market Time' forces had intercepted nine major attempts at infiltration and had captured six trawlers, each carrying tons of arms and ammunition.

Another particularly valuable contribution made by U.S. naval forces engaged in coastal operations was gunfire support. In May 1965 a Naval Gunfire Support Conference was held in Saigon to coordinate the use of such fires in support of the Vietnamese Army's operations ashore. Following this conference, 'Market Time' ships were tasked with providing naval gunfire support as part of their routine responsibilities. However, most of the requirements for such support were met by ships of the Seventh Fleet. On 20 May 1965, an American destroyer, the USS *Hammer*, fired the first such support mission. By the end of that year, ships of the Seventh Fleet had fired 90,000 projectiles against communist targets ashore. The true effect of these fires was not always easily determined. However, on 15 December 1965 the destroyer USS *McKean* fired 292 5-inch shells at Viet Cong forces attacking a Vietnamese Army outpost. The American advisors with the Vietnamese ground units reported later that the ship's fire had stopped the communist attack and accounted for sixty-nine of their dead. By 1968 such support had become a normal feature of ground combat in coastal areas. This can be appreciated from the contents of one monthly report that accounted for 860 fire missions resulting in the destruction or damage of 425 junks offshore and 745 structures inland.

Junk crew of Coastal Group 32 board and search a fishing junk near Vung Tau in January 1966. Note the presence of the U.S. advisor. (USN)

U.S. Marine outpost in I Corps area, 1966. The U.S. Marines, able to receive their logistic support over the beaches or through secondary ports, were committed to the I Corps area of Vietnam where the infrastructure was less developed than in the south. Thus, when the need arose for a ground component to join with the navy to form the Mekong Delta Mobile Afloat Force, no marine units were available and the assignment went to the 9th Infantry Division of the U.S. Army.

U.S. Marine Corps amphibious cargo carrier M76.
This 5 ton vehicle could carry ten men or 1½ tons of
cargo over 200 kilometers in soft ground or swampy
areas. The marines in I Corps experimented with the
M76 but found their standard tracked landing vehicle
LVTP(5) adequately met their operational requirements inland.

Opposite
U.S. Marines of Company 'A', 3rd Amphibian
Tractor Battalion on the beach of the Batangan
Peninsula during Operaton 'Dragonfire' in the
Quang Ngai Province of Annam in September 1967.
It should be noted that the marines published a draft
doctrine for riverine operations (FMFM 8–4) in
1966 which addressed only equipment organic to the
U.S. Marine Corps and hence had only limited
applicability to the 'joint operations' conducted by the
U.S. Army and Navy in III and IV Corps areas.
The doctrine did provide guidance for the conduct of
small scale riverine operations in I Corps. (USMC)

U.S. Marine LVTP(5), a lightly armored tracked
amphibious vehicle of 37 tons able to carry 34 troops
or 5 tons of cargo. This vehicle represented the end
product of a progression of tracked landing vehicles
that began with the LVT1, first used in the assault
landing on Guadalcanal Island by the First Marine
Division, 7 August 1942. The LVTP(5) was well
used in the many amphibious operations the marines
conducted along the coast of Annam. (USMC)

Amphibious operations were also conducted separately wherein the capabilities of the landing force to move ashore
by boat, amphibious vehicle, or helicopter provided a choice of landing sites and
varied schemes of maneuver ashore that
often threw the enemy off-balance. The
first opposed landing, Operation 'Star-
light', conducted on 18 August 1965
clearly demonstrated the exceptional
flexibility that an amphibious operation
provided. In that operation, a helicopter-
borne assault and a river crossing by
amphibian tractor were coordinated with
an over-the-beach landing in the first
regimental-level landing of the Vietnam
War. The operation was particularly successful and resulted in just under a
thousand enemy dead in six days. Less
successful was Operation 'Deck-house V'
in January 1967, which marked the first
time that American combat forces entered the Mekong delta. Unfortunately,
the operation was based upon poor intelligence and suffered accordingly.

American brown water naval operations along the coast of South Vietnam
included amphibious landings in addition to the routine patrol and fire support
missions already discussed. Many of
the sixty-two landings conducted by
U.S. forces from 1965 to 1969 involved
the Amphibious Ready Group/Special
Landing Force (ARG/SLF) of the
Seventh Fleet. However, other landing
force units also were used. Most often
these were U.S. Marine Corps units from

the Marine III Amphibious Force deployed ashore in I Corps area. Beginning
with Operation 'Blue Marlin' in November 1965 units of Vietnamese Marines
were occasionally embarked and the very
last SLF operation, conducted on 7 September 1969, had South Korean Marines
augmenting the American landing force.

The more successful amphibious operations were those where the landing
force was used to exploit the maneuver of
a ground force operating on land.

Command relations in the execution of amphibious operations were complicated by amphibious objectives often being located in operational areas already assigned to friendly forces ashore and offshore. This complication applied equally to air operations. The attendant problems were resolved by special agreements that allowed operations to proceed outside the provisions of formal amphibious warfare doctrine. It was perhaps fortunate that fifty-three of the sixty-two landings took place in I Corps area, where most of the American units were U.S. Marines already well accustomed to working closely with navy counterparts.

Although the last U.S. amphibious operation of the Vietnam War took place in 1969, there were four landings made in 1972 using U.S. amphibious forces and Vietnamese Marines that warrant attention. These occurred when North Vietnamese troops crossed the 17th parallel and drove the defending South Vietnamese back toward Hue. On 13 May

1972 two battalions of Vietnamese Marines were landed from ships by helicopter to positions behind the enemy formations. This was a highly successful tactic and was repeated on 24 May when two battalions again were landed by helicopters and one battalion by amphibian tractors. Two final landing operations followed, one on 29 June and the last on 22 July. These final landings were almost all made by helicopter, reflecting the pattern of operations that had come to characterize the amphibious assault as practised at the end of the war.

There were no classic beach assaults during the Vietnam War. The emphasis, rather, was placed on using rotary-wing aircraft for the ship-to-shore movement and landing without opposition. Moreover, every effort was made to land the maximum number of troops in a single lift. One helicopter squadron was considered capable of a single such lift of 600 men. The single-wave operation was complicated, but it denied the enemy the

opportunity of concentrating fire on each of the successive waves that had characterized earlier assault techniques. For this reason the single-wave operation was preferred despite the difficulties its execution might engender.

The Naval Advisory Group under MACV had evolved from the Navy Section of the former MAAG. Its functions, as its designation indicated, remained solely advisory in nature. In 1965, the Group had 750 U.S. personnel of whom four-fifths were serving as advisors, 300 with Vietnamese naval forces in the field. Each ship of the Sea Force had an advisor embarked. Other advisors were with the Junk Groups of the Coastal Force, the Assault Groups of the River Force, and the Vietnamese Marines.

When, in 1965, 'Market Time' responsibilities were passed to MACV from the Seventh Fleet, the forces involved were formed into a separate Coastal Surveillance Command (TF 115) to reflect their operational functions. Then, when the

U.S. Navy later established an inland patrol organization to parallel that of 'Market Time', the two operational commands were placed, in April 1966, under a Commander, Naval Forces, Vietnam who separately retained title as Commander, Naval Advisory Group. The timing of these developments suggests that the priority given to coastal waters by the U.S. Navy was dictated by circumstances and not by any lesser concern for events inland.

The U.S. Navy had also been following the situation in the delta. It was already supporting the Vietnamese Navy in the Rung Sat, the area of dense mangroves that covered the access to Saigon from the sea, in a sustained effort to clear the area of communist forces. It was aware that the Vietnamese River Force was seldom available for routine patrolling and that the capabilities of paramilitary and other security forces for this task were limited at best. Accordingly, in September 1965, the U.S Navy established its own river patrol force. This was code named 'Game Warden' and, as Task Force 116, was the second operational command placed under the Commander, Naval Forces Vietnam. 'Game Warden' began operations on 11 February 1966.

The mission of 'Game Warden' forces was to conduct river patrols and inshore surveillance to enforce the curfew and prevent Viet Cong infiltration. Patrol operations were conceived from the outset as a combined U.S.-Vietnamese effort. Experience gained in the Rung Sat revealed that American patrol boats manned by mixed U.S.-Vietnamese crews worked very well. However, this arragement could not be repeated for 'Game Warden' because the Vietnamese military personnel were not available. Accordingly, National Police or paramilitary personnel were embarked for liaison and interpreter duties.

Patrols were normally made up of two boats operating within radar range of one another. Daylight patrol zones were some 50 kilometers long and were covered by the boats moving in loose column at varying speeds. Specific routes as well as time of patrols were randomly selected. Since traffic was generally dense it was impossible to check all boats but the high speed of the patrol boats made a

Above
A river patrol base showing the rectilinear arrangement of the base and the use of water as a barrier to enemy movement.

Below
A Coastal Force base's inland defenses. Note how close the defenses are to the boats.

substantial sampling of the traffic possible. At night all boats underway were in violation of curfew. These were immediately pursued and seized or destroyed as circumstances required.

Patrol tactics were intended to minimize interference with lawful traffic. Still, at the beginning, patrols were viewed with some concern by the local populace. But, as time went by, the security that followed upon the patrol effort became increasingly appreciated. This positive reaction of the people was counter to communist interests and led to greater hostility. The lightly armored patrol boats were vulnerable and depended pri-

marily on their speed to withdraw beyond weapons range when fired upon. Sniper fire was usually ignored but evasive action was promptly taken when heavier fire was received. At times the boats would reply with grenade launcher of machine-gun fire against established Viet Cong positions. More often, however, helicopter gunships or artillery were called in.

The enemy moved at night. The patrol effort was intensified accordingly. Within a section of ten patrol boats, two would undertake a daylight patrol while six would be used at night. With patrols lasting twelve to fourteen hours, the patrol area was adequately covered. Then, as patrols gained experience they were used to support Vietnamese River Force operations or to insert and extract special raiding groups in communist base areas.

The 120 patrol boats initially required by 'Game Warden' were modified commercial sport craft. These were ordered from the American builders in November 1965 and when modified were designated PBR Mark I. The craft were 9.5 meters in length and had a draught of under 50 centimeters. They had a fiberglass hull and were propelled at up to 25 knots by two waterjet pumps. They mounted three .50 caliber machine-guns and one 40 mm grenade launcher. They also had two radio receivers and one radar. Half a

ton of armor plate covered vital areas. The first of these boats were delivered in January 1966 and by the end of that year all 120 boats were on patrol in South Vietnam. An additional eighty boats were ordered in March 1967. These, slightly larger and with the forward twin .50 caliber machine-guns relocated toward the bow were designated PBR Mark II.

Probably the most difficult of the many problems associated with 'Game Warden' was that of basing the boats. 'Game Warden' initially involved four PBR divisions, each of three sections with ten boats. Later, when the eighty PBR Mark II arrived, six new sections were added to the existing divisions and a new fifth division of two sections was formed. The basing plan initially was to keep the boats no more than 35 nautical miles from their patrol areas. On that premise it was envisaged that three floating offshore bases and eight permanent inland bases would be required. In time the LSTs used as offshore bases were augmented with floating workshops. The number of ashore bases also were increased as operations along the Cambodian border were undertaken. Still, facilities were never more than marginally adequate. To make matters even more difficult, it was not always possible to integrate satisfactorily the defense of the

Observation post of base defense system. Unless well covered by protective fires, such posts were very vulnerable.

river boat bases with those of local forces. 'Game Warden' energies and resources necessarily had to be diverted to the defense task accordingly.

The use of LSTs as afloat bases was a welcome innovation. The ships could hoist PBR on board for maintenance. They themselves could proceed directly to rendezvous with supply ships and thereby avoid transshipment complications. Most important, LSTs provided their own defense and relieved patrol boat units of this added burden. The major disadvantage of the LST bases was their offshore location. This had been decided upon because LSTs were thought to be too vulnerable to be stationed on inland waters. But, when the monsoon season arrived, the utility of the LSTs was so reduced that the risk of moving them inland was accepted. There, it was soon learned, they could perform their base tasks without undue hazard. This discovery led to the use of LSTs as mobile bases to extend the range of 'Game Warden' activities.

'Game Warden' was an effort confined to the major waterways. Countless canals and narrow streams could not be searched on a regular basis. The PBR

LST 1161, Vernon County *modified into a self-propelled barracks ship (APB) for use by the Mobile River Force. Note monitors and armored troop carriers on port side, LCU on starboard side and Sunday religious services being held on the bow.* (USN)

U.S. Navy patrol aircushion vehicles (PACV) on patrol in Plain of Reeds area. (USN)

were very noisy and did not appear to offer significant advantages over the already available helicopters. 'Game Warden' did prove effective but the challenge of extending its capabilities remained until the end.

In 1965, when the United States began to commit combat forces in South Vietnam, the Viet Cong had 70,000 troops in the Mekong delta. These were organized to provide one guerrilla squad per hamlet, one guerrilla platoon per village, one separate company per district, one battalion per province and corresponding reserves at the regional level. The objective of these forces was to eliminate the presence of the government in the countryside and destroy the South Vietnamese military organization. This was to be accomplished initially by gaining control over the central delta provinces to isolate Saigon, and then radiating outward to seize the remaining peripheral provinces. The communist forces were generally well trained, professionally led, and adequately armed. Moreover, they had numerous bases throughout the delta, many of which had never been disturbed and were available to support operations in the IV Corps area and adjacent III Corps area.

The delta, except for Long An province and the Rung Sat, lay within the IV Corps area, where the 7th, 9th and 21st Vietnamese Army divisions reinforced by five Ranger battalions and three armored cavalry regiments were deployed. These units totalled 40,000 men. In the same corps area the Vietnamese Navy had six of its River Force Assault Groups and eleven of the Coastal Force Junk Groups. In addition, there were a number of regional and popular force units. These, regrettably, had poor morale and high desertion rates due in some part to their armament being inferior to that of the Viet Cong.

The Americans, that same year, had deployed the 13th Combat Aviation Battalion to the delta. That powerful unit, made up of four assault helicopter companies and one reconnaissance airplane company, was extensively used in support of Vietnamese Army opera-

A patrol air cushion vehicle (PACV) makes an intercept. This air cushion vehicle was 12.2 meters long and weighed 5 tons and was capable of up to 55 knots. It could carry 2 tons or up to 20 persons including its crew. (USN)

were too vulnerable to commit to such areas and surveillance was limited to what could be accomplished by helicopter units or occasional Vietnamese Army patrols in assault boats. In the search for improved means to cover the more remote delta areas, the Americans experimented with air-cushion vehicles, notably the British-made SRN-5. This six-ton hovercraft performed well, particularly in the Plain of Reeds, but they

Mobile Riverine Force Operations: Schematic Concept

The Mobile Riverine Force (MRF) comprised afloat facilities able to accommodate a reduced army brigade of two infantry battalions, two river assault squadrons each with some fifty specialized craft, and several repair, maintenance and supply ships. The mobile river base (MRB) could be anchored up to 50 kilometers from an area of operations but was normally much closer. Security for the afloat base was to be provided by monitors and assault support patrol boats (ASPB) on the river flanks of the base. Infantry detachments of platoon strength were to be deployed on the opposing banks of the waterways to cover the land flanks of the anchorage.

Operations were usually of the search and destroy type and were planned to encircle the enemy to ensure his destruction. This required the movement of infantry units by watercraft and helicopters. Reserve units were to be held afloat or were to be positioned near helicopter pickup zones ashore. Ground units were to be deployed into blocking positions either before or during the search phase; monitors and ASPBs were to cover the flanks of the waterborne force's landing sites and block enemy waterborne movement. Fire support was to be provided by assault force boats, by artillery emplaced on barges or ashore, by helicopter gunships and by fixed-wing tactical aircraft.

It was planned that the army component of the MRF would remain embarked for up to six months. It was also planned that the afloat base location would be shifted every four to six weeks and that tactical operations would extend over five days with a three day interval for rest and equipment servicing. In practice, it was found that the afloat base location had to be shifted more frequently and that tactical operations lasting beyond two days resulted in a severe deterioration in personnel effectiveness.

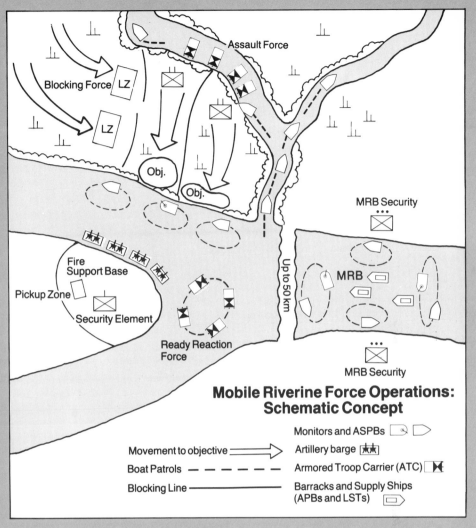

Mobile Riverine Force Operations: Schematic Concept

Movement to objective ⟹
Boat Patrols – – – – –
Blocking Line ――――

Monitors and ASPBs
Artillery barge
Armored Troop Carrier (ATC)
Barracks and Supply Ships (APBs and LSTs)

tions. There were also almost 3000 American advisors attached to Vietnamese military units. Among these was the legendary Lieutenant Dale Meyerkord USNR, the advisor to Vietnamese Navy River Assault Group 23. Meyerkord had found in the RAG commander, Nguyen Van Hoa, a man who shared his dynamism and intense interest in the task at hand. Together they became a team which quickly earned the respect of the Viet Cong. Meyerkord, who was liked and equally respected by the Americans and Vietnamese with whom he worked was killed on 16 March 1965. It was the thirtieth time that he was in a boat that received hostile fire.

At the beginning of 1966 allied strength in the delta reached 150,000. This was double the numbers of Viet Cong, but the preponderance was deceptive. The Viet Cong represented a relatively cohesive organization. The allied units, in contrast, ranged from well motivated and battle-tested regulars to unreliable village militia. It is not surprising under these circumstances that fully a quarter of the population was under communist control and that much of the remainder was subject to intimidation, harassment, or worse. Indicative of the communist power was the decline in rice tonnage reaching Saigon markets. The delta always had been a rice exporting area; in 1966 the Americans had to begin importing rice into the country.

'Market Time' had been established to help deny access to South Vietnam from the sea to the communists. 'Game War-

A monitor leads a formation of ATCs as River Assault Division 92 sets off on an operation in the Mekong delta area in June 1968. (USN)

Right
US Navy armored troop carriers (ATC) land troops of the 2nd Brigade, U.S. Infantry Division in one of a succession of river assault operations conducted in July 1967 in Con Giouc district. In July 1967 a succession of riverine assault operations were carried out in the area to the west of the Rung Sat. These resulted in 316 Viet Cong being killed, 15 captured and 68 weapons seized. In these actions the re-supply of the riverine force was carried out by helicopter directly from the supply LST. This was the first time this had been attempted. The practice was adopted as standard practice whenever feasible thereafter since it eliminated multiple handling of supplies and expedited delivery to the combat units. (USN)

den' was being built up as rapidly as possible to assist in policing the major waterways inland. These were positive and necessary actions. But MACV believed more American forces were needed: 'Market Time' and 'Game Warden' were specialized operations and did not have the offensive power the situation in the delta appeared to require.

The desirability of moving American combat forces into the delta had already been advocated by MACV in 1965. In that year, it had become evident that, while the Vietnamese there were able to hold their own, they were not by themselves able to reduce the communist grip over the land and the people. By early 1966, the question was no longer whether or not to send troops to the delta but where to base them.

American staff officers had visited IV Corps area to study the basing problem and had reported that no open land was available. The only options that would permit an early deployment of U.S troops were to have them share already overcrowded Vietnamese Army facilities or displace civilians. Neither of these alternatives was acceptable. Attention was then turned to the possibility of

Mobile Riverine Force Landing Operations

MRF landing operations were similar to those of the French but differed vastly in the means used. The Americans made regular use of artillery, and rotary and fixed-wing aircraft. The French had no helicopters for such purposes and few fixed-wing aircraft; French air strength in 1954 was three squadrons of B-26 and four fighter/attack squadrons. Their artillery was equally limited; out of 683 pieces in Indochina in 1954, half were in fixed positions and the remainder heavily committed. In American MRF operations three sections, each with one monitor and three ATCs, were used to embark the assault platoons of an infantry company. The movement to the landing area was made in column; boats in a section kept 5–10 meters apart while 150–300 meters were maintained between sections. The formation was preceded by ASPB minesweepers immediately followed by the command boat (CCB) with the senior naval commander; the landing force commander was also embarked or might be overhead in a helicopter. When the formation approached to within 500 meters of the landing area any artillery fire or air strikes were lifted. The ASPBs and monitors picked up the responsibility for continuing the preparation, while the ASPBs took

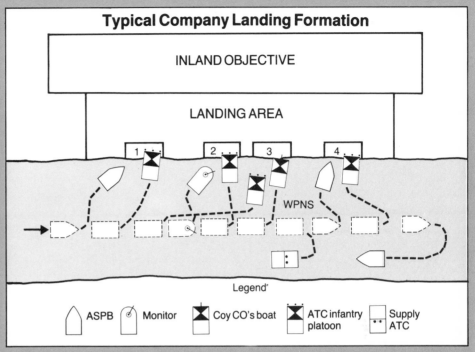

position on the flanks of the landing area. The ATCs would then execute a turn into the shore and land the assault platoons, which promptly moved inland. Accompanying supply ATCs would take station off the landing area, prepared to land on call. As soon as the assault troops made contact with the enemy ashore, the landing force commander maneuvered his uncommitted forces into blocking positions by boat and helicopter and

took the enemy positions under heavy fire by all available means; the assault force then closed in to finish him off. When boats had to remain in the operational area overnight, they were moved close to the shore where the infantry could assure their security; the boats' weapons were integrated into defense fire plans. Once the operation was concluded the troops would re-embark in the same boats and return to base.

---

dredging sufficient fill to create a base area. The additional dredges required were ordered but would not be available until late in 1966. The only possibility remaining to help move matters forward was to use a floating base, and this idea had taken hold by the beginning of 1966. The concept of the Mekong Delta Mobile Afloat Force (MDMAF) evolved shortly thereafter.

It was envisaged from the first that an additional U.S. Army division would be sent to South Vietnam. Two of its three brigades were to be based ashore; one at Vung Tau and the other near Mytho. The third brigade was to be based afloat. In the proposal forwarded by COMUSMACV on 15 March 1966,

the afloat base was to comprise five self-propelled barracks ships (APB), two LSTs, two harbor tugs (YTB) and two landing craft repair ships (ARL). Tactical mobility was to be provided by river assault squadrons each capable of lifting a battalion. The river assault squadrons were each to have twenty-six LCM-6 as armored troop carriers (ATC), two command and control boats (CCB), five LCM-6 as monitors, sixteen assault support patrol boats (ASPB) and one LCM-6 refueler. A salvage force made up of two heavy lift craft, two tugs, two LCU and three floating dry docks was to serve the base.

The operational concept presented in the plan provided for the basing of the

army component on barracks ships for a period of six months. The embarked brigade would rotate with those ashore as arranged. The base would be located in a hostile zone where it would remain for four to six weeks before shifting to a new operational site. Tactical operations would be conducted at distances of up to 50 kilometers from the base. Such operations would normally last about five days after which three days would be allowed for rest and the servicing of equipment. It was estimated that in this manner one battalion could systematically search an area of 40 square kilometers during each tactical operation.

The movement of forces involved in a tactical operation was to be made by

Opposite
Assault support patrol boats (ASPB) cover the land-
ing of US Army units from armored troop carriers
(ATC) in a mobile riverine force operation in the
Mekong delta in December 1967. (USN)

Right
Monitors and assault support patrol boats with
elements of the 4th Battalion 47th Infantry on Song
Ba Lai, April 1968. On 4 April 1968 a typically
vicious engagement occurred on the Song Ba Lai in
Kien Hoa Province. As River Division 92 with the
2nd Battalion, 47th Infantry embarked entered the
water-way it suddenly received very heavy rocket and
automatic weapons fire. Company B in ATCs with
accompanying ASPBs drove through the 'killing
zone' and landed above the enemy. Company E,
which according to the battalion counter-ambush
standard procedure should have landed below the
enemy, actually landed in his immediate vicinity. A
costly and confused fire fight ensued. The 4th Battal-
ion was ordered in to assist and by nightfall the
enemy force had been driven off. The following morn-
ing the sweep continued without further contact. (US
Army)

Right
Troops of the 60th Infantry, U.S. 9th Infantry Divi-
sion landing from an MRF armored troop carrier
(ATC) north of Ben Luc during operation Coronado
IV. This operation took place from 19 August to 9
September 1967. In the early phases of the operation
the 3rd Battalion, 60th Infantry under control of the
2nd Brigade moved by boat from the base on the Soi
Rap River, below Saigon, up the Vam Co Dang
River. It landed north of Ben Luc where it caught an
enemy force by surprise. The Viet Cong driven into
the open were attacked by helicopter gunships and 34
were killed. This phase of the operation ended on 22
August and accounted for 59 enemy dead at a cost of
only six Americans wounded. (US Army)

Opposite
Armored troop carrier supported by an assault
support patrol boat lands a combat patrol. Com-
bat patrols were routinely used to sweep through
cleared areas to ensure that the enemy had not returned.
Most of these patrols encountered no resistance;
any area known or suspected of harboring Viet Cong
units was promptly attacked by river or helicopter
assault forces and not by combat patrols. Still, on
occasion, a routine patrol found itself in a brief but
deadly fire fight. (USN)

Early Riverine Operation in Dinh Tuong Province (IV Corps Area)

In May 1967 Vietnamese Army intelligence reported four major Viet Cong bases in the Cam Son area of Dinh Tuong Province. The U.S. 2nd Brigade planned a search and destroy operation to eliminate these bases using two battalions of infantry supported by twenty-two ATC, two monitors and two CCBs of River Flotilla One. A brigade command post and barge-mounted artillery were prepositioned near the operational area. At 0815 hours on 15 May the 3rd Battalion, 47th Infantry (3/47) landed at the mouth of the Rach Ba Rai. Thirty minutes later 4/47 landed two companies just west of the Rach Tra Tan. The troops moved inland and the boats took station to interdict possible enemy moves. At 1200 hours Company A of the 4th Battalion, 47 Infantry (A4/47) was airlifted from Dong Tam base to a position 3 kilometers north of the Mytho River and west of the Rach Tra Tan. At 1400 hours the two landing companies of the 4th Battalion (B4/47 and C4/47) made contact with a strong VC force and further progress became very difficult. Company A was ordered to move south while the reconnaissance platoon of 3/47, held afloat, attempted to penetrate into the Rach Tra Tan to land on the enemy flank; it was driven off by heavy fire. By 1630 hours the enemy was observed to be moving to the northeast. One company of 3/47 was airlifted into blocking positions at 1700 hours but no contact was made. At 2000 hours, after all firing had

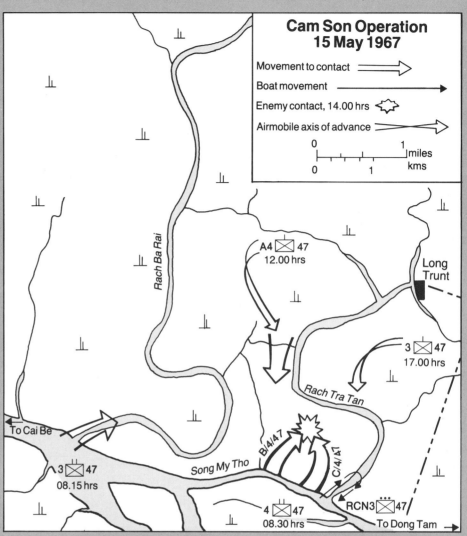

Cam Son Operation 15 May 1967

Movement to contact
Boat movement
Enemy contact, 14.00 hrs
Airmobile axis of advance

0 —— 1 miles
0 —— 1 kms

ceased, the action was broken off. This operation emphasized the difficulties of maneuvering boats in restricted waterways, particularly in periods of low water. It also revealed the vulnerability of troops in assault boats to rocket fragments. Lastly it vividly demonstrated the elusiveness of the enemy and his ability to break off an engagement and disappear into the countryside. These problems became regular features of MRF operations.

land, water and air. All operations were to be coordinated with local forces; 'Game Warden' forces, for example, were to be used for reconnaissance and intelligence. Maximum use was to be made of air support and artillery was to be echeloned in conventional fashion to support all phases of the tactical operation. During movement on the waterways the ASPBs would cover the flanks and rear of the formation and join the monitors in providing close-in fire support. The

monitors would lay down preparatory fires on landing sites assisted by air and artillery as specified in the fire support arrangements. Once a landing was made the river boats could be used to seal off possible enemy withdrawal routes. The afloat base was to maintain operating levels of rations, dry cargo, fuel and ammunition. Resupply was to be handled by LSTs sailing between the base and Vung Tau where a support command was to be established. In this

manner, the afloat base would be independent and have no impact on the local economy.

Despite this last point, the Vietnamese generals commanding major forces in the delta were not pleased at the prospect of having a large American force operating in their area. Meanwhile, the MACV proposal was moving up the chain of command at a deliberate pace. General Westmoreland, convinced of the seriousness of the situation in the delta, sought

Armored troop carriers and assault support patrol boats prepare to land elements of the 2nd Brigade, 9th U.S. Army Infantry Division east of Mytho; note supporting ASPB in center of formation. From 10 to 12 April 1968 the Mobile River Force condcuted a succession of operations near the towns of Vinh Kim and Long Dinh, east of Mytho, to clear the area of Viet Cong. Few enemy were encountered. However, the barracks ship USS Benewah and one supply LST were hit by rocket fire while at anchor in the base area. Damage to the ships was minor, but an LCM refueler that also was hit was destroyed. (US Army)

There nonetheless remained reservations among Americans as well as Vietnamese over the introduction of U.S. combat forces into the delta. The embassy in Saigon, for one, identified potential problems arising from such a deployment. The embassy stated in late September 1966, that there was the possibility that a U.S. presence in the delta would encourage the Vietnamese military to cease their own efforts there. It was also possible that increased military activity would destroy rice producing areas, increase the already serious refugee problem, and incite violent communist reactions against population centers. The Department of the Army itself suggested on 27 September an expanded advisory effort as an alternative to the MDMAF. But these concerns were voiced almost two months after the decision had been made by Secretary Mc-Namara and the MDMAF was well on the way to becoming a reality.

On 1 September 1966 the U.S. Navy created River Assault Flotilla One (Task Force 117) and River Support Squadron 7 in the United States. Then, in November, River Assault Squadron 9 and River Assault Squadron 11 were activated. These units began their training in California. In January 1967 RAS 9 elements began arriving in Vietnam and continued their training in the Vung Tau area. Meanwhile the first elements of the 9th U.S. Infantry Division had reached Vung Tau in December and were able to join in the navy's training. This was short lived for on 16 February 1967 the 3rd Battalion, 47th Infantry and River Assault Division 91 were ordered to disrupt enemy activity in the Rung Sat. A Viet Cong attack on a freighter moving through the Rung Sat on its way to Saigon had caused MACV to interject a touch of realism to the first joint navy-army exercises.

In January 1967, the Dong Tam base being dredged near Mytho had sufficient area to receive one battalion of the 9th Division. A second battalion was provisionally based at an airfield eight kilometers northeast of Mytho. These troops engaged in local operations, not the least of which was the defense of the growing Dong Tam base whose presence had become of particular interest to the Viet

to accelerate matters. He emphasized to his superiors the importance of denying the resources of the delta to the Viet Cong and the corollary stabilizing effect on the rice economy that friendly control over the whole of the delta would have. By mid-1966, when a scaled-down version of the plan had received approval of the American Secretary of Defense, Westmoreland had also reversed the negative attitude of the Vietnamese generals.

Opposite
Assault support patrol boat engaged in supporting a routine combat patrol is hit and damaged by surprise enemy fire. The boat is run ashore while the crew attempt to determine the extent of the damage. (USN)

Field expedients: *Elements of the 34th Artillery, 9th US Infantry Division seen on an artillery barge of the Mobile Riverine Force. The deployment of artillery units by boat to support riverine operations was hampered by the limited number of suitable landing sites and firing positions ashore. In the latter part of 1966 the US Army's 3rd Battalion, 34th Artillery developed a barge able to accommodate two 105 mm howitzers fixed in firing position. Six such barges were built at Cam Ranh Bay. For operations, the barge was towed by an LCM-8 to a river bank within range of the operational area where it was securely anchored to the shore. These artillery barges saw extensive service in the Mekong delta as part of the American riverine force. (U.S. Army)*

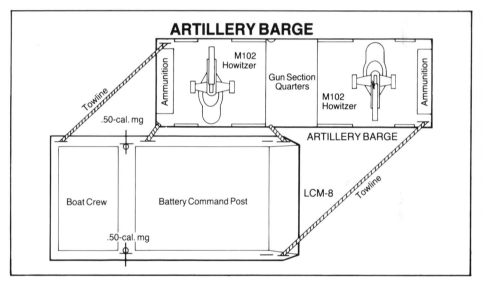

ARTILLERY BARGE

Airmobile artillery firing platform used for a 105 mm howitzer of the 4th Artillery, 9th US Infantry Division. These platforms could be emplaced and leveled in shallow water but, while effective, were less versatile than the barges. (US Army)

Opposite
US Navy units of the Mobile Riverine Force (Task Force 117) beach along a waterway of the Mekong delta to unload US Army troops and stand by to provide covering fire as required and recover the force on termination of the operation. ASPBs would normally be covering the flanks of the formation while the troop carriers are beached. Note external 'Venetian blind' armor to detonate shaped charge projectiles before reaching main armor. (USN)

U.S. Army helicopter evacuates wounded during operation 'Coronado' V. This operation launched on 12 September 1967 involved riverine assault operations north of the Mytho River. On 15 September the 3rd Battalion, 60th Infantry moved up the narrow Rach Ba Rai and encountered heavy enemy machine-gun and rocket fire. In replying to this fire and in supporting the landing and subsequent operations ashore during the first twelve hours of the action, the boats expended over 10,000 rounds of 40 mm and proportional amounts of 81 mm mortar, .50 and .30 caliber machine-gun ammunitions. The operation, which lasted four days, cost the Americans and supporting Vietnamese 16 dead and 146 wounded; the enemy lost 213. (USN)

Cong. The U.S. Navy followed the army to Dong Tam where, in April, RAS 9 had been assembled. Further joint training was undertaken until 2 June when the afloat base became operational. This, as decided by Secretary McNamara, had only two of the five APB requested. The serious shortage of army berthing places was remedied in part by the navy providing a barracks barge (APL) and a larger LST. In this manner it became possible to base two battalions afloat and thus restore some balance to the MDMAF. The first afloat deployment was made on 11 June 1967.

The creation of a modern river force involved innumerable problems of organization and equipment. Each of these was complicated by the novelty of the operational concept and the lack of experience. It was true that the French and Vietnamese had eatablished the essential elements of a valid concept. However,

the scale they had used was conditioned by limited resources and was much more modest in scope than the Americans had envisaged. A further complication was the absence of a doctrine for river warfare that was agreed by the parties soon to be engaged in the endeavor.

The French had handled matters informally; their navy ran the boats and the Expeditionary Corps HQ decided where they would be used. The same attitude and acceptance of operational realities were adopted by the American at the field operations level. At the higher echelons, however, the absence of prescribed relationships and responsibilities was troublesome. One of the more important differences was that the army viewed operations of the MDMAF as an extension of 9th Division responsibilities. The navy, on the contrary, believed the afloat force should be fully independent and able to deploy as the military situa-

second year of its existence, the MRF was confined largely to pacification tasks in one province and in the last months of its existence it progressively lost the assets that had enabled it to function as an effective strike force.

The life of the MRF appears to have passed through three phases. During the first six months the MRF had conducted sustained operations against main enemy forces in the northeastern IV Corps and adjacent III Corps areas. The Vietnamese forces in the delta at that time had been widely dispersed so as to extend a minimum of security to population centers and along major roads and waterways. Accordingly, Vietnamese offensive capabilities were limited. The MRF, whose army component could maneuver by water and by air, was a welcome reinforcement. Admittedly, an airmobile brigade could have been equally welcome in the conditions then existing, but the added capability provided by the river assault squadrons enabled penetration of waterways that heretofore had been the exclusive domain of the Viet Cong.

These were rewarding areas for the MRF to operate in. The Viet Cong, believing itself secure in its base areas and as yet unfamiliar with the power and flexibility of the MRF, suffered major losses. The MRF had prepared itself well for deep penetrations beyond artillery range by devising barges upon which artillery could be mounted and towed into support positions. It had not, however, been prepared for the debilitating effect of the riverine environment on men and equipment. Where the initial MDMAF concept had envisaged tactical operations lasting five days, their duration was soon reduced to two days followed by one day of rest. The shifting of the base location took place every ten to fourteen days rather than every six weeks as originally planned. Another finding during the first six month period was that the success of MRF operations most often depended upon the employment of other forces such as shore-based units of the 9th U.S. Division or the Vietnamese Marines.

tion required. This issue was softened somewhat when on 31 January 1968 the Mobile Riverine Force (MRF), as the MDMAF had come to be called, was placed under the operational control of the senior American advisor in IV Corps.

The U.S. Marines had published an interim doctrine for riverine operations (FMFM 8–4, Tentative) in April 1966 which addressed only Marine Corps organization and equipment. It could not apply in the situation under consideration where the navy was to play a rôle equal to that of the ground force. The U.S. Navy had no published guidance on the subject and neither did the U.S. Army. However, Lieutenant General Victor Krulak, commanding the Fleet Marine Force Pacific (FMFPAC), had foreseen that an analysis of the French experience in Indochina could well serve to guide a future American involvement in such operations. A study responding

to that view was prepared and published in March 1966. Its contents specifically addressed the conduct of joint riverine operations in terms of existing amphibious warfare doctrine (NWP 22) and strongly influenced the army's TT 31–75 'Riverine Operations', published in 1967. This document, while not approved by the U.S Navy, was the only 'official' guidance available when the MDMAF became operational and was extensively used. The navy's own doctrine for riverine operations (NWP 21), equally influenced by the FMFPAC study, did not appear until 1969 when the riverine force was about to be disestablished.

The MRF operated from June 1967 to June 1969. It had been conceived to carry on offensive operations against major Viet Cong units throughout the delta. That capability was successfully exploited, notably in the northeastern provinces during the first year. In the

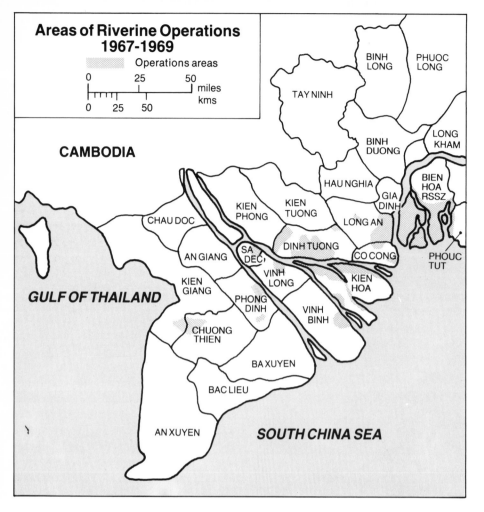

Areas of Riverine Operations 1967-1969

Operations areas

0   25   50 miles

0   25   50 kms

CAMBODIA

GULF OF THAILAND

SOUTH CHINA SEA

BINH LONG

PHUOC LONG

TAY NINH

BINH DUONG

LONG KHAM

HAU NGHIA

GIA DINH

BIEN HOA RSSZ

CHAU DOC

KIEN PHONG

KIEN TUONG

LONG AN

CO CONG

PHOUC TUT

AN GIANG

SA DEC

DINH TUONG

KIEN GIANG

VINH LONG

KIEN HOA

PHONG DINH

VINH BINH

CHUONG THIEN

BA XUYEN

BAC LIEU

AN XUYEN

The second phase of the MRF's operational life began with the Lunar New Year (Tet) of 1968. When the communists launched their countrywide Tet Offensive at the end of January, the MRF was dispersed at several locations along a major waterway to serve as fire support bases. The immediate problem was to gather in all these elements and reassemble the force. The Viet Cong tried to interfere but failed. Then, when the MRF was ordered to assist heavily engaged allied forces near Mytho, the Viet Cong again tried to block its passage and again failed. When, later, the pressure against Mytho lessened, the MRF was deployed to a blocking position some 25 kilometers away, from where it was moved to Vinh Long on 4 February. Finally, on 8 February it was directed to the vicinity of Saigon where it remained until the communist effort collapsed.

The pattern of operations that followed was a succession of small scale actions. These were unlike the multi-

battalion engagements of the earlier period and reflected the unwillingness of the Viet Cong to engage large units after the losses sustained during their Tet operations. Still, the Viet Cong were no less aggressive against the MRF. This was evident in the increased numbers of ambushes encountered and the increased numbers of casualties being inflicted by communist 'hunter-killer' teams.

The tactical operations undertaken by the MRF after the Tet Offensive continued the practice of close association with other forces, either Vietnamese or American. But the enemy appeared less eager to confront a large force and such operations were eventually discontinued. The last of these took place in August when the MRF deployed into the U Minh forest some 85 kilometers southwest of Cantho. This was the first major allied force to enter that area in more than ten years and its ten days duration was one of the longest tactical operations undertaken.

The third and final stage found the MRF centering its activities in the Kien Hoa Province in a multiplicity of operations associated with pacification. The period was accompanied by numerous changes in the organization of both the army and navy components of the MRF. It also marked the gradual decline in U.S. Army participation in riverine operations in favor of increased use of Vietnamese forces and a shift in operational emphasis to interdiction operations.

The inability of the MRF to embark a third battalion and the commitment of that unit to the defense of the Dong Tam base had caused the afloat brigade to work extensively with Vietnamese units. This had worked well and had helped lessen the earlier concern over the possible adverse effects of a foreign presence in the delta. By mid-1968 the navy had finally received its third river assault squadron. This should have enabled the army to complete its afloat force. However, the withdrawal of the third battalion from Dong Tam required the 9th Infantry Division to adjust its base security missions. This the division would not do until the completion of the review being made of the organization of the division's tactical units for riverine operations. While this matter remained under consideration, the 2nd Brigade was assigned Kien Hea province as its main area of operations. Eventually the third battalion was made available but because of the limited waterways system in the province the added afloat facilities could not be accommodated and the battalion was based ashore.

In September a fourth river assault squadron arrived in Vietnam in company with several more barracks ships. This made it possible to organize two Mobile River Groups. The force in Kien Hoa province became Group Alpha and continued its operations in that area. Group Bravo was deployed in the central delta to undertake an interdiction program. By November, elements of these two Groups were operating independently. Of the five river assault divisions in Group Alpha, one each was assigned to support the 3rd Vietnam Marine Battalion; the 3rd Battalion, 34th Artillery; the 3rd Battalion, 60th Infantry; and the 3rd Battalion, 39th Infantry. The fifth

Mobile Riverine Force Operation in Can Giouc District (III Corps Area)

In mid-1967, a succession of operations in the Can Giouc District had cleared out over 300 Viet Cong and captured sixty-eight weapons. On 20 July, further action was initiated by the 3rd and 4th Battalions, 47th Infantry (3/47 and 4/47) which departed their afloat base at daybreak in ATCs and sailed west on the Vam Co River. Company C of the 4th Battalion (C4/47) was landed at Fire Base X-Ray to remain as reserve with three ATCs. At 0700 hours the remainder of the force landed on a 4 kilometer front on the east bank of the Song Rach Cat 3/47 to the north, 4/47 on the south. The troops moved east toward the Song Nha Be making slow progress across the rice paddies. The brigade and battalion commanders were airborne directing operations; air force forward air controllers and artillery observers also kept the area under close surveillance. By 1000 hours the troops had advanced 2 kilometers while the boats followed ready to provide supporting fire if needed. At 1030 contact was finally made with a strong force which was promptly taken under fire by the supporting artillery. By 1100 the air force had joined in and was delivering 750-pound bombs and napalm on the enemy positions. The American ground units continued to maneuver to encircle the enemy while the monitors and ASPBs of the river force covered the flanks of the advancing infantry. By 1300 all maneuver elements were in place; at 1415 the reserve from Fire Base X-Ray was airlifted into a blocking position and by 1515 the encirclement was completed. The net was tightened during the afternoon. By nightfall seventeen VC dead had been found; the following

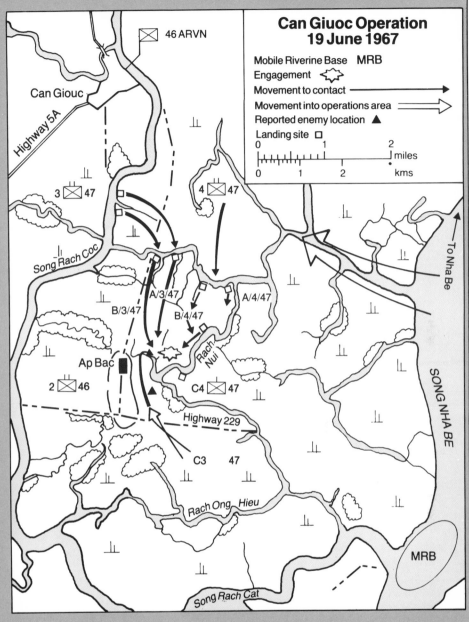

morning when the area was finally swept fifteen more were found and ten prisoners were taken.

This operation was an excellent example of the successful utilization of the complementary capabilities of the U.S. Army, Navy and Air Force in difficult terrain, while executing a complicated maneuver in the presence of a hostile force.

river assault division was assigned to base defense duties. Of the three river assault divisions assigned to Mobile Riverine Group Bravo, one was on base defense duty, another was on interdiction operations and the third supported the 4th Vietnamese Marine Corps Battalion.

The pattern of widespread operations continued on into the new year. In January 1969 the U.S. Navy began the transfer of assets under the Vietnamization program. This program to turn the war over to the Vietnamese gradually was to gain in importance; in June alone sixty-four boats modified for riverine assault operations were given to the Vietnamese Navy River Force. In other matters the U.S. Navy was becoming increasingly involved in 'Sealords' operations.

In the fall of 1968 Vice Admiral Elmo Zumwalt became Commander, Naval

A U.S. Navy PBR engaged in 'Sealords' operations lands a patrol along a waterway near the Cambodian border.

June 1968. The operational environment in the Mekong delta reduced the effectiveness of troops ashore. It also adversely affected arms, ammunition and equipment, June 1968. (USN)

Early Riverine Operation in Long An Province (III Corps Area)

In mid-June 1967 the newly formed MRF left Dong Tam for Vung Tau. There it received the additional boats needed to bring the flotilla up to fifty-two ATC, ten monitors, four CCB, and two refuelers (note: the ASPBs authorized where not yet available and the ATCs had to perform ASPB missions). From 13 to 17 June the MRF performed routine operations in the Rung Sat. It then moved into Long An province where on the evening of 18 June it anchored within 3 kilometers of a remote Viet Cong base area in Can Giouc district. During that night one Vietnamese infantry battalion (2/46) moved by trail into blocking positions south of Ap Bac village. Early on the morning of the 19th, five U.S. infantry companies landed from assault boats and began to sweep southward; a 6th U.S. infantry company (C3/47) moved by boat to a reserve position near an air pickup zone. At 1000 hours Vietnamese intelligence reported a Viet Cong force of battalion size opposite the Vietnamese infantry battalion blocking position. The reserve U.S. infantry company (C3/47) was airlifted at 1105 hours south of the reported enemy position, while one of the unengaged U.S. infantry companies (C4/47) was ordered to move by boat and land northeast of the reported enemy. The airlifted company swept the area without making contact. However, the company landing from boats encountered heavy fire, as did one of the initially committed companies (A4/47) moving south. The enemy force had been found but it was northeast of where it had been reported. The

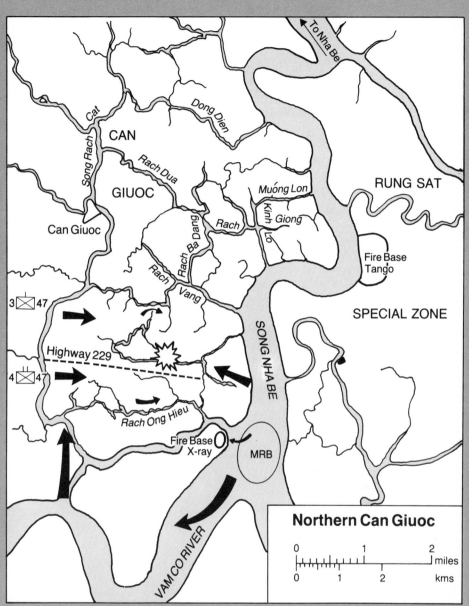

American commander then maneuvered his companies to close on the enemy while striking at him with all available artillery, air, and boat gun fire support. Boats also took up blocking positions on the adjacent waterways. By 2000 hours, darkness and enemy fire brought an end to further friendly force movements. At dawn on 20 June, when the Americans resumed their sweep, the enemy had disappeared.

Forces Vietnam. That officer, later to become Chief of Naval Operations, fully supported the Vietnamization program initiated in the closing days of President Johnson's administration. Upon his arrival in Saigon, Admiral Zumwalt promptly established ACTOV (accelerated turnover to Vietnam) to lend impetus to the transfer of military assets to the Vietnamese. ACTOV was a systematic program that began first with the training of the Vietnamese in the operation and maintenance of the equipment they later were to receive. Admiral Zumwalt also found that an intelligence analysis confirming the importance of Cambodia as a major logistics base for the communists in Vietnam underscored the validity of Operations 'Sealords' whose primary purpose was to clear and hold key delta areas.

During the Vietnam War the communists extended their use of Cambodia as a haven and base area. To prevent the movement of communist forces and supplies along the waterways that cross the border the U.S. Navy undertook 'Sealords' operations. By that time, the U.S. Army was also engaged in land operations along the same border, but farther east. They had made incursions into the Plain of Reeds and had fought several engagements in the nearby 'parrot's beak', where Cambodian territory projects deep into Vietnam.

On 15 October 1968 the U.S. Navy established Task Force 194 at Can Tho to conduct 'Sealords' operations. The main object of these operations was to form a deep barrier below the Cambodian border to interdict the flow of supplies to the communists from the Cambodian safe haven. A second and closely related purpose was to establish friendly control over the trans delta canal system that linked the branches of the Mekong River.

'Sealords' operations made use of all available assets. Initially these involved units of the 9th Infantry Division but soon more and more Vietnamese were engaged. It is significant that the commander of the coastal surveillance force 'Market Time' was responsible for 'Sealords' operations carried on from the sea, while the commander of the river patrol force 'Game Warden' was responsible for large scale strike operations on the inland waters. Equally significant is the mission related designation of the subordinate commands within TF 194. These were identified as the Coastal Raiding and Blocking Group, the Riverine Raiding and Blocking Group and the Riverine Strike Group.

A measure of the accomplishments of the 'Sealords' campaign is to be found in the results of the barrier operations initiated respectively on 2 November, 16 November, 6 December 1968 and 2 January 1969. In these four operations, 164 tons of ammunition and 386 tons of military supplies were seized; there were also 331 enemy captured and 2788 confirmed enemy dead. The most rewarding of the operations was 'Giant Slingshot' conducted in the 'parrots beak', the

'Sealords' operation in Ca Mau area. Vietnamese Marine patrol landing from a 'Market Time' 'Swift' boat. It was operations in such environments that caused the US Army to decide that troops ashore should be relieved every two days rather than every five days as had first been thought possible. (USN)

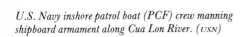

U.S. Navy inshore patrol boat (PCF) crew manning shipboard armament along Cua Lon River. (USN)

'Sealords' operation in Ca Mau peninsula area. Vietnamese Marines as shown embarking on 'Swift' boats after a sweep ashore. (USN)

Cambodian salient in III Corps area pointing at Saigon. The violent reaction of the communists confirmed the importance of the area as a major line of communications. This operation also marked a deviation from the afloat base concept. Because the ships normally used for an afloat base could not be brought in to the area, large flat barges were substituted upon which temporary base facilities were built.

The year 1969, so well begun, continued to register substantial military progress. The accelerated pacification campaign went well and large areas, once communist dominated, passed under government control. Riverine forces contributed significantly to this achievement and, in so doing, provided valuable experience for both Americans and Vietnamese. In mid-year the Vietnamization program was sufficiently advanced to allow the withdrawal of the 9th U.S. Infantry Division and its return home. Shortly thereafter River Flotilla One was disestablished. With that ended

the Mobile Riverine Force; that powerful offensive organization created to bring the war to the enemy and destroy him passed into history.

The war, however, was far from over. Bilateral peace talks between the Americans and Hanoi had begun in early 1968 and had shifted to quadripartite talks to accommodate all parties concerned the following year. Still, the war appeared to have a momentum of its own. The South Vietnam government at long last had declared general mobilization and its military establishment soon passed one million men. Then the war was extended into Laos and Cambodia. By 1970, after two years of peace talks, the Vietnam War was becoming a second Indochina War. Two more years were to elapse until on 27 January 1973 the Paris Accords brought a cease fire to the devastated land.

For a few months there was the promise of real peace but in 1974 the communists played their final card. Early in the year they began a series of probing

attacks designed to test the determination of the South Vietnamese and the interest of the Americans in returning. The Vietnamese, uncertain over their ability to fight without the direct support of American units they had come to rely on, faltered and then broke. The Americans, torn by Watergate and domestic discord wrought by the war, did not return. The outcome was inevitable; South Vietnam collapsed and on 30 April 1975 the North Vietnamese entered Saigon.

At the height of the Indochina War a French statesman had demanded it cease being a French war supported by Vietnam and become a Vietnamese war supported by France. Fifteen years later the United States had reached the same conclusion in regard to its involvement. The American effort was to prove no more successful than that of the French. But, the span of time from the return of the French to Indochina to the departure of the Americans from Vietnam confirmed again the importance of brown waters and of the navies needed to hold them.

US Coastal and Riverine Forces, 1965–1969

U.S. Navy Coastal Surveillance, South Vietnam 1965 – 'Market Time'

By early 1965 the Americans had concluded that infiltration from the sea was taking place in junks mingling with the normal inshore traffic and from larger ships paralleling the coast far offshore and turning shoreward only to reach discharge points ashore or transfer points closer inshore. To counter this activity the Vietnamese were maintaining sixteen Sea Force ships on patrol and up to 190 junks of the paramilitary Junk Force on station near major traffic lanes offshore. To improve this effort, five Coastal Surveillance Centers were established in March to coordinate operations and the Seventh Fleet was tasked with conducting offshore surface and air patrols. By May, when U.S. ships received authority to board and search suspect craft in Vietnamese territorial waters, there were eleven Seventh Fleet ships engaged in the effort and sufficient aircraft to maintain a continuous air patrol over the whole coast some 70 kilometers offshore.

On 20 July, eight U.S. Coast Guard cutters (WPB) arrived at Danang. Eleven days later nine more of these 82-foot, 20-knot boats arrived at An Thoi. These boats, eventually to number 26, were used for inshore barrier patrols below the 17th parallel and off the Vietnam-Cambodia border. The 64-ton boats were armed with a .50 caliber machine-gun over an 81 mm mortar forward and two 20 mm guns aft.

At the end of July, command of the U.S. Coastal Surveillance Force, TF 115 (code name 'Market Time') passed to the U.S. Military Assistance Command, Saigon. At the same time the first of the new fast 'Swift' boats arrived in-country. These 25-knot craft were armed with twin .50 caliber machine-guns forward and the dual .50 caliber machine-gun/81 mm mortar aft. Crew armament included a light machine-gun plus a 40 mm grenade launcher. A total of 84 of these boats were in operation by the end of 1966.

The coast of South Vietnam was divided into nine patrol areas (see map on page 95). Each patrol area was assigned to one of the Seventh Fleet ships, normally, either an ocean minesweeper (MSO) or a radar picket escort (DER). Additionally, the two border patrol areas were covered by coast guard patrol boats (WPB), while the inner seven patrol areas were covered by the Swifts.

U.S. Coast Guard Patrol Boats (WPB). These 25.2 meter boats of 65 tons were able to do 17 knots. The Americans used them to maintain inshore barrier patrols below the 17th parallel and off the Cambodian border.

Fifty foot Swift boat used for inshore coastal surveillance. The Swift first came to Vietnam in October 1965. (USN)

U.S. Navy 'Neptune' patrol aircraft off the coast of South Vietnam conducting 'Market Time' operations in coordination with USS Leader, Ocean Minesweeper (MSO 490). (USN)

U.S. Navy River Patrol Force, South Vietnam 1965 – 'Game Warden'

The organization of the U.S. Navy's Coastal Surveillance Force (TF 115, 'Market Time') was paralleled by the creation of a river force in September 1965 to patrol inland waterways, to deny them to communist insurgents and enforce the curfew. This U.S. Navy River Patrol Force, code name 'Game Warden', was designated Task Force 116 and placed under the naval component of the U.S. Military Assistance Command, Vietnam. 'Game Warden' forces were initially organized into a River Squadron of four divisions each with ten patrol boats (PBR). These 120 boats corresponded to the number established as necessary for an effective patrol of the major waterways. The operational concept envisaged PBR patrolling in pairs over a 50 kilometer stretch of water during a 12-hour period; night patrols were to be three times more frequent than daytime patrols. Within the first year of operations a further requirement for 80 additional boats was generated.

The U.S. Navy had no boat available to meet the 'Game Warden' requirement. Further, the press of time precluded going through the usual design, prototype, test and procurement process. Thus, reference was made to the commercial boat market where a boat was found that corresponded in general to the performance characteristics desired. On 29 November 1965, a U.S. Navy contract was awarded to the United Boat Builders of Bellingham, Washington, for 120 PBRs; an additional 40 were ordered in February 1966 for training use and as replacements. These 9.5-meter boats had fiber glass hulls and used water-jet propulsion. They were capable of speeds up to 25 knots. The first was delivered in January 1966 and an initial increment reached Vietnam two months later. By April, PBRs started patrolling inland waters in Vietnam and by December all 120 boats were on station. Then on 29 March 1967 another contract was awarded to the same company for 80 more PBRs. These, designated Mark II, reflected operational experience gained in the previous months. They had 1000 kilograms greater displacement and were slightly larger than the Mark I. The most

evident difference was that the .50 caliber machine-gun mount in the Mark II was slightly farther forward than in the Mark I.

The speed with which the PBRs were deployed was quite remarkable. Far less reassuring was the base situation in Vietnam. The initial idea had been to base PBRs within 70 kilometers of their patrol areas. This required three offshore bases and eight inland bases. But the boats arrived faster than base facilities could be provided with the result that other facilities had to be used. The first two bases were at Cat Lo and Nha Be. Then, in 1966, five more bases were established in delta towns. At the same time, plans were made for two additional bases near the Cambodian border. When these were ready in early 1967, one of the original five delta bases was shut down.

Difficulties did not end with the completion of the shore bases; once built, they had to be defended. Wherever possible shore base defenses were integrated with local security forces. But, ultimate responsibility remained with the 'Game Warden' units. The use of bases afloat greatly simplified this problem. The three LSTs that were assigned quickly demonstrated their usefulness not only in terms of defense but also in support of all phases of 'Game Warden' operations. The first LST arrived in November 1966 and soon thereafter all three ships were on station off the mouths of the major delta rivers. Operations proceeded smoothly until the onset of the summer monsoon when the ships had to enter the rivers if they were to continue their support activities. It was soon learned that they were far less vulnerable than had been feared; eventually, LSTs serving as PBR mobile bases were operating from inland waterways within 30 kilometers of the Cambodian border. Then, in time, other afloat base facilities were built on shallow draft 'Ammi' pontoons which could be towed into position and assembled into platforms on which the base units could be mounted.

It is useful to add that whereas 'Market Time' units were used in tactical operations in inshore areas, 'Game War-

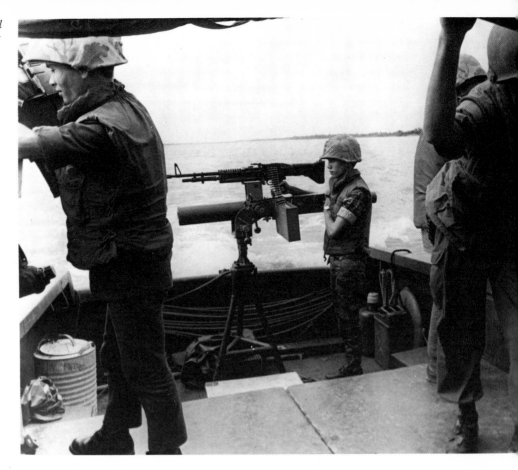

PBR Mk I on patrol on the Cau Dai River, 11 April 1969. These fiber glass hull boats, propelled by water jets were capable of 25 knots. They were armed with twin .50 caliber machine-guns forward and a .30 caliber machine-gun aft. (USN)

A U.S. Navy air-cushion vehicle on patrol in the Plain of Reeds.

den' forces were used for surveillance and intelligence gathering in support of riverine operations, but did not participate directly in such operations. They did, however, work closely with the U.S. Navy's Sea, Air, and Land units (SEAL). These highly trained units were tasked with counter-guerrilla and intelligence gathering missions of a covert nature. 'Game Warden' boats, able to operate silently at night, were often used to insert and recover the six to ten man SEAL teams that were used in such operations.

While the U.S. Navy found the PBRs able to meet the basic needs of a river patrol force, it kept alert to other types of craft for this mission. Among those considered were air cushion vehicles. A number of these were brought in-country in 1966 and used in the Plain of Reeds. They proved effective insofar as their mobility was concerned but were demanding in the maintenance required and they were extremely noisy. The question of their relative utility as compared to the helicopter was never answered in full; the fact ACVs remained experimental craft provides some clue.

144

U.S. Mobile Riverine Forces, South Vietnam

The Mekong Delta Mobile Afloat Force (MDMAF) was conceived originally as being made up of an infantry brigade and sufficient armored river craft to conduct assault operations from an afloat base complex. As eventually organized, the Mobile Riverine Force (MRF) could only accommodate a reduced brigade of two infantry battalions, reinforced, (2nd Brigade of the 9th U.S. Infantry Division) and the boats of River Flotilla One. This last was made up of River Support Squadron Seven and River Assault Squadrons Nine and Eleven. Included in the RAS were a total of 52 armored troop carriers (ATC), ten monitors, four command and control boats (CCB), 32 assault support patrol boats (ASPB) and two LCM refuelers.

The MRF as constituted engaged in riverine operations from June 1967 to June 1969. Additional river assault squadrons and base ships were deployed during that period, but because assets were being transferred to the Vietnamese as the Vietnamization program gained momentum, the basic structure of the MRF remained essentially the same throughout its existence. After June 1969 the U.S. effort in the delta was controlled principally by Task Force 194 under the code name 'Sealords'. Operations of TF 194 in fact had started in the latter part of 1968, when 'Sealords' had been launched with the primary object of blockading Cambodia by interdicting the inland waterways. 'Sealords' operations made use of 'Market Time', 'Game Warden', and MRF resources together with Vietnamese rangers, marines, and other local units and were conducted into 1970.

The fleet of U.S. river assault craft, with the exception of the ASPBs, were modified LCM-6s. These 17.5-meter boats were first designed for amphibious assault operations, where they could be loaded with one tank, or other combat vehicles and equipment, or up to 120 troops. For brown water operations, they had to be heavily armed and armored. The battleship of the river forces was the monitor. In this type of river craft the ramp forward was replaced by a rounded bow behind which a 40 mm cannon was

Above
Armored troop carrier with helicopter pad (ATCH) of the Mobile River Force. (USN)

Below
Armored troop carrier of the Mobile River Force. (USN)

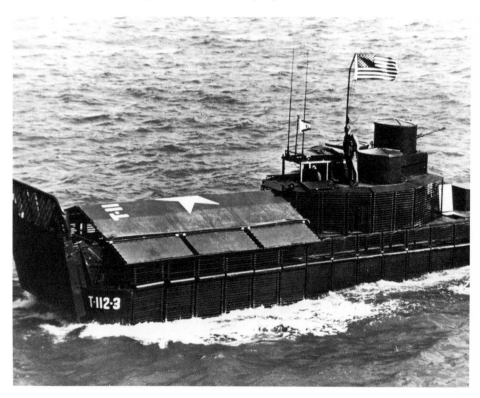

mounted in a turret; some later models mounted a 105 mm howitzer instead. The other monitor armament included one 20 mm cannon and two .50 caliber machine-guns aft and two .30 caliber machine-guns midships, where was also located an 81 mm mortar. A number of these boats had their forward armament replaced by a flame thrower. These boats retained two 20 mm cannons

and had a flame device able to project up to 1000 liters of napalm to a range of 150 meters. All monitors had an eleven man crew.

The command and communications boat (CCB) aslo had an eleven man crew and resembled the monitor. The main visible differences were the number of antennae and that the mortar well of the monitor was covered over in the CCB to provide added accommodation for electronic equipment. The armored troop carriers (ATCs), with a seven-man crew, retained their bow ramp. They were armed with one 20 mm cannon and two .50 caliber machine-guns aft. Some later models also carried a 40 mm grenade launcher. In time most ATCs were also fitted with a helicopter platform that enabled them to serve as floating medical aid and evacuation stations. In its tactical transport role an ATC normally embarked a reinforced infantry platoon of 40 men.

The 15.4-meter ASPB was specifically designed for riverine operations. With its five man crew and speed of 16 knots, it was the scouting element of the river

force. Its forward 20 mm cannon, midship .50 caliber machine-gun and aft mounted mortar enabled the ASPBs to serve also for fire support. Finally, it was equipped with minesweeping gear to add further to its capabilities.

The mobile river base (MRB) initially comprised two barracks ships, one repair ship, two supply LSTs and a small salvage force. The barracks and repair ships were modified LSTs whose shallow draft and general configuration were well suited to the brown water environment. The afloat base also made use of pontoons to facilitate boat operations. These were later adapted as artillery platforms and to provide base facilities in areas where larger ships could not penetrate.

Opposite right
Converted LST Benewah *used as barracks ship of the Mobile Riverine Force in the Mytho area.* (USN)

LCM modified into a monitor armed with 40 mm and 20 mm guns and 81 mm naval mortar. (USN)

Command and communications boat of the Mobile River Force. (USN)

Opposite below
LST converted into river craft repair ship (ARL) with armored troop carriers (ATC) awaiting servicing and repair. (USN)

Assault support patrol boat. A high speed armored boat used for interdiction, escort, surveillance, minesweeping and fire support. (USN)

Mobile Riverine Force Operations, 1967–68

The Mobile Riverine Force (MRF) was an American organization. However many of its operations were carried out in conjunction with those of Vietnamese units and all MRF operations were routinely coordinated with Vietnamese commands. Moreover, a great deal of the intelligence upon which the MRF acted was received and disseminated by Vietnamese military and provincial authorities, particularly informant reports.

MRF operations ranged widely over the delta area of South Vietnam in 1967 and 1968. Most frequent were operations in the northeastern IV Corps Area, with occasional extensions into the adjacent III Corps Area. That general area was heavily infested with Viet Cong forces which sought to isolate Saigon from the resources of the delta and from its access to the sea (see map an page 134).

The Concept of the MRF as a self-contained strike force able to operate in remote delta areas was well implemented the first year, 1967. The main effort in that period was made in the Long An and Dinh Tuong Provinces. Strike operations were also conducted in Go Cong and Kien Hoa Provinces. The Rung Sat Special Zone lying between Saigon and Vung Tau was an area of intense and continuing activity; its location made it well suited to provide combat orientation to new arrivals.

At the time of the communist Tet Offensive in early 1968 the MRF was used to relieve the pressure against the populous towns of Mytho, Cantho and Vinh Long. Later in the year, MRF operations were again concentrated in Long An, Dinh Tuong and Kien Hoa Provinces. At this same time, U.S. Navy 'Sealords' operations began and carried on into the following year, bringing the war into the Plain of Reeds and the more remote western provinces.

Bottom
An ASPB (assault support patrol boat) of the American Mobile Riverine Force patrols off a landing site where helicopters are bringing in an artillery battery. (USN)

The UH-1 helicopter was an essential complement of the American Mobile Riverine Force.

148

Right
Minesweeping gear. Four minesweepers were developed for use on the brown waters of Vietnam; the MSB, a wooden hull, 30-ton boat; the MSR, a modified 30-ton ASPB; the MSM, a modified 70-ton monitor; and the MLMS, a converted U.S. Navy standard 50 foot (15.4 meter) motor launch.

Below
River assault force embarked in armored troop carriers (ATC) departing the mobile base off Dong Tam area. (USN)

'Sealords' Operations South Vietnam

The Mobile River Force had as its army component a brigade of the U.S. 9th Infantry Division. The division itself had a tactical area of responsibility and controlled the support assets, notably the helicopters, upon which the afloat brigade depended on a regular basis. The circumstances tended to maintain the center of gravity of the MRF in the northeastern part of the delta. Thus, as additional resources became available, the U.S. Navy began to use them to establish an inland blockade of Cambodia, from where supplies were being infiltrated to the Viet Cong. This was the genesis of 'Sealords' operations. In time, these operations were extended to gain control over the major trans-delta waterways and to clear the Ca Mau peninsula area.

'Sealords' operations were conducted with any and all brown water resources; most often this involved U.S. Navy river craft and Vietnamese Marines. 'Market Time' assets were generally used in operations near the coast; thus 'Swift' boats (PCF) and the Vietnamese Marine Corps were the forces engaged in the Ca Mau area. MRF navy elements with Vietnamese marine or army units participated in operations farther inland. After the 9th Division was repatriated and the MRF was dis-established in

mid-1969, the U.S. Navy assets not transferred to the Vietnamese were retained for 'Sealords'.

In 1968 the Americans started their Vietnamization program whereby their in-country forces began transferring their assets to the Vietnamese. The Vietnamese thenceforth assumed ever-increasing responsibility for the conduct of military operations. When, in 1975, this effort collapsed and the communists gained control over the whole of Vietnam, they captured a very substantial naval establishment. Among the booty now held by the communist Vietnamese Navy there are:

- 26 U.S. Coast Guard patrol boats (WPB).
- 107 SWIFT inshore coastal patrol boats.
- 293 PBR river patrol boats.
- 84 assault support patrol boats (ASPB).
- 42 monitors, MK 5 (built as monitors in 1969).
- 22 monitors, modified LCM 6.
- 100 armored troop carriers, modified LCM 6.
- 8 command and control boats (CCB).
- 27 river patrol craft (RPC).

This sizeable force represents one of the largest brown water navies in existence today.

'Sealords' operation in Ca Mau area. Vietnamese Marine patrol about to land from 'Market Time' 'Swift' boats in restricted waterway. (USN)

'Sealords' operations to clear the Ca Mau peninsula area made use of 'Swift' boats from 'Market Time' forces and Vietnamese Marines. A patrol cautiously enters a narrow waterway in the area during a March 1969 operation. (USN)

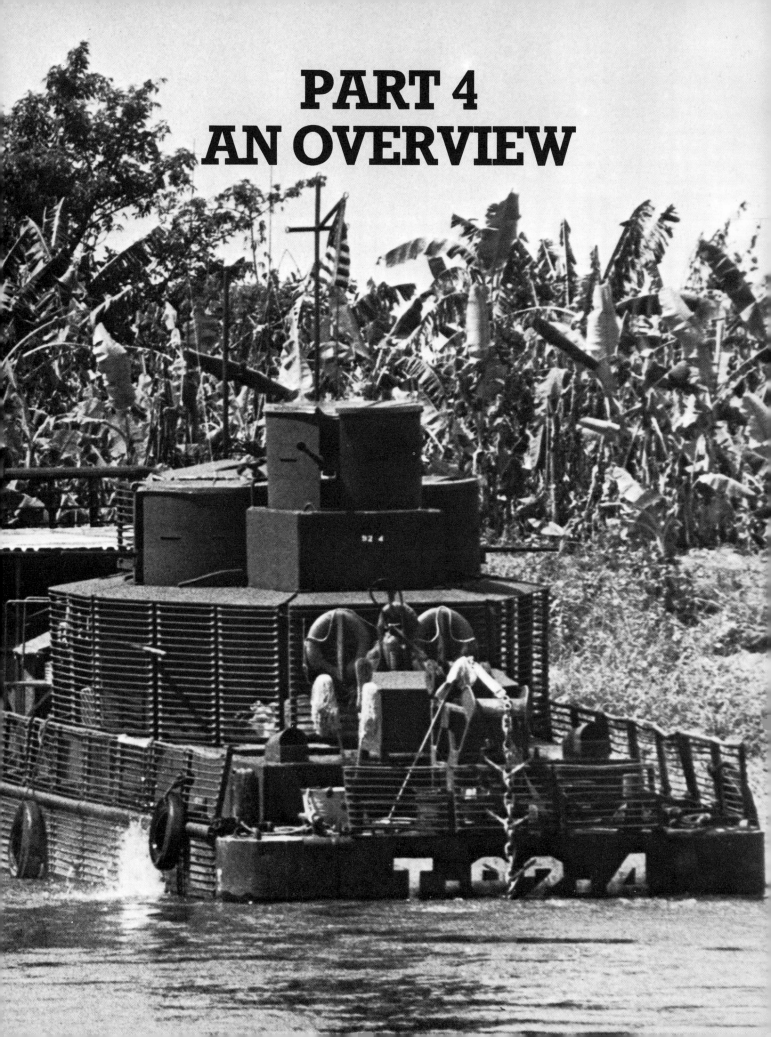

PART 4
AN OVERVIEW

10
Summation

The establishment of the Japanese in Tonkin in 1940 was followed by an era of turmoil and violence throughout Indochina that still smolders today in Cambodia. The intensity of the struggle has varied greatly over the years. Varied also have been the issues and the protagonists involved. Political and economic matters, or even military affairs beyond those concerned with brown water warfare, are outside the scope of this narrative. Still, tactics support strategy and the story of brown water warfare in Indochina, essentially a tactical matter, has its origins in a strategy rooted in political issues which need mention if only for background.

The French lost Indochina to the Japanese. Then, in 1945, when Japan found itself nearing defeat, it allowed local governments to proclaim their independence. This was shortlived in the case of the Kingdoms of Laos and Cambodia which readily accepted the return of the French as overlords later that year. However, the Vietnamese proved unyielding and eight years of war followed. This, for the French, started as a colonial war. But, when China fell to Mao Tse Tung in 1949 and the Korean War started in 1950, the Indochina War became a struggle against communism.

While the subtleties of the Indochina War were learned with time, the French soon found that the struggle required two types of forces: static and mobile. The static forces were those needed to clear areas of dissident elements and restore an administration able to counter sources of dissatisfaction. They also had to maintain control over the roads and waterways that made economic activity possible and enabled the extension of government authority. The other basic type of military force was exemplified by the brigade-sized 'groupes mobiles', whose mission was to seek out and destroy the enemy's main battle formations.

The resources available to the French for these tasks were not only inadequate but also required extensive adaptation. The French had brought into Indochina conventional divisional units, the 3rd and 9th Colonial Infantry Divisions and the 2nd Armored. These were too cumbersome and had to be fragmented. But even when that was done, the units reorganized for combat in the deltas were not equally well suited to fight in the highlands. Further, the effectiveness of any given organization varied with time as well as place. Thus, the 'groupes mobiles' with their three battalions of infantry, one battalion of artillery, and 120 vehicles were successful in the deltas and lowlands as long as the roads and waterways needed for their movement were secure. When, in 1953, such security was no longer available, the 'groupes mobiles' had to commit a large part of their infantry to safeguard their communications and their effectiveness suffered accordingly.

The difficulties associated with fixed territorial forces were no less challenging. Although two thirds of the infantry in Indochina was committed to static duties, this still fell short of requirements. The nature of the problem can be appreciated from the situation in 1953, when over 82,000 troops were immobilized in posts scattered over the Tonkin delta at a time when Viet Minh strength within the same area approximated only 35,000. Despite this disparate ratio of static forces to enemy numbers, no post could ever be expected to hold in the face of a determined attack. Because of such realities, the French concluded that tying down troops in isolated posts did not ensure control of communications unless the area had first been sanitized. They then replaced the system of posts by one of fewer but well defended bases able to support mobile operations.

Among the more effective organiza-tional innovations of the French were the naval assault divisions, the 'dinassaut' of the navy and the amphibious groups of the army. The eight dinassauts, each with two patrol boats, two command and fire support boats, and a transport element of six modified landing craft, were too few in number and too lightly equipped. Each could embark an infantry company and, with added transport, could accommodate an infantry battalion. But they lacked organic infantry elements of the strength needed to give them an independent strike capability. As a result, the dinassauts were most often used in supporting roles and as defensive forces.

All rivercraft activity in Indochina was coordinated with the navy. Thus, the navy had cognizance over the operations of the eight platoons of LCM in the army's Transportation Corps and over the activities of the boat patrol units of the armored cavalry. But all such units, including the dinassauts, were based within army territorial commands. Moreover, the dinassauts, other than for routine patrolling, were invariably used in support of army units. These command arrangements were simple and worked well. However, they did little to help the dinassauts acquire their own offensive capabilities. The French Navy command did recommend on several occasions the assignment of infantry units to the dinassauts. But the army did not have enough units to spare for specialized duties, although it did make available a number of commando-type formations for such purposes.

There was the further fact that the limited numbers of rivercraft did not permit the simultaneous movement of large troop units. When these were required, the boats had to operate a shuttle service. Then, too, parachute units were often used in conjunction with riverine operations to close the trap on an enemy

154

force. The success of such operations depended upon the location of suitable drop zones and the possibility of rapid intervention. Unless the paratroops were already airborne and the drop zones identified in advance such operations required time to organize. This meant delay and this reduced the chances of success. Helicopters would have simplified the task but these were never available in the numbers needed.

In short, the dinassaut emerged as an organization of great potential, but its value was never fully realized simply because the resources were not there. One may also surmise that the fortunes of the dinassaut were not advanced by subordination to an army command waging a difficult war that required innumerable adaptations and innovations for its prosecution.

Another asset never fully exploited was the control of the sea enjoyed by the French Navy. Coastal operations were rare and generally limited to raids. Again, this was largely a question of means. The ships best suited for amphibious operations were few and many of the landing craft had been adapted to meet the hazards of riverine warfare and could no longer safely serve in ship-to-shore operations. Moreover, troops were not trained for such operations. It was only in late 1953 that an amphibious training center was opened at Cam Ranh Bay. This prepared the units engaged in Operation 'Atlante', an amphibious operation launched in 1954 to regain control over central Annam. But, by then, the war was largely over for the French.

The amphibious group of the army did not appear until 1953. Its component elements, however, had been operational for several years before. The light weight amphibious tracked cargo carriers called 'weasels' by the Americans and 'crabs' by the French had demonstrated their utility from the start. After that, it was largely a question of applying combat lessons as they were learned. This was done first by organizing 'crabs' into tactical units to provide them mutual support. Then, infantry was added to protect the vehicles better and serve as a maneuver element. But the 'crabs' were limited in their carrying capacity. Attention was then turned to the larger amphibian tractor, the LVT, able to carry up to thirty troops and also serving as a gun platform. The combination of the 'crabs' serving as a scouting force integrated with troop-carrying and cannon-firing LVTs made for a powerful autonomous strike force whose effectiveness in delta areas was unmatched. Two amphibious groups, each built around an infantry battalion and a battery of mobile artillery, were eventually formed.

The French adapted their military organization, equipment, and tactics to the unconventional nature of the conflict and the imperatives of the terrain, as best they could. They also came to the conclusion that the Vietnamese would have to take on a greater share of the burden of the war. Thus, in addition to recruiting Vietnamese for the Expeditionary Corps, the French in 1950 set about creating the Vietnamese Armed Forces. This effort, dynamically endorsed by General de Lattre, was directed overwhelmingly at the organization of a land army.

The French naval authorities in Saigon fought against this submergence of a Vietnamese naval identity and also differed with Paris over the initial structure the Vietnamese Navy should take; Paris wanted to include blue water units from the first but Saigon argued that the Vietnamese should start with a river navy. The Saigon naval authorities also planned to organize a Vietnamese Marine Corps made up of small infantry units trained to serve with river units. In all these matters the Saigon view eventually prevailed, but this took time. A naval training center was started at Nha Trang in 1951, but the first Vietnamese Navy unit, the *Cantho* Dinassaut was not formed until April 1953. This unit had only one command LCM and a transport element of two LCM and two LCVP. But it did fly the Vietnamese flag. A second similar dinassaut was formed in June of the same year.

The year 1953 marked the beginning of a Vietnamese Navy. It also marked the establishment of a General Staff and a single defense budget. This was unfortunate for the two-dinassaut navy because its insignificance as compared to the army was certain to see it ignored. This apprehension, first voiced by the French Navy, was well founded. The Vietnamese Navy eventually reached a strength of over 13,000 men by 1965 but it never gained a position of authority on the General Staff.

The Vietnamese Marine Corps had an even more precarious start as a scattering of small units serving as adjuncts to the river force. The survival of the marine corps and its eventual growth into a 6000-man brigade by 1965 was due to the influence of U.S. Marine Corps advisors who, beginning in 1955, were able to fuse its constituent elements into battalion-size units and have the General Staff accept them, together with the army's parachute regiment as the nation's general reserve. The performance of these units in combat fully justified the wisdom of these actions.

The Indochina War ended in 1954 with the Vietnamese Navy operating four dinassauts, each able to embark one rifle company. Then, as the French began to withdraw from the country, additional assets became available and many of these were transferred to the Vietnamese. As a result, a sea force appeared in 1955 and a fifth dinassaut was added to the river force that same year. Further, the lift capability of the dinassauts, thenceforth called river assault groups (RAGs) was increased by several LCM and LCVP.

Despite these developments the Vietnamese Navy lacked the means to patrol the coast effectively. The addition of a paramilitary force of sea-going junks to cover inshore areas beginning in 1960 helped but little. On the rivers, in contrast, the RAGs were more powerful and more numerous than the French dinassauts that had preceded them. But the small infantry units that had served in the dinassauts under the French had been used to form the 1st and 2nd Vietnamese Marine Corps Battalions. The RAGs, bereft of organic infantry elements and under Vietnamese Army command, found themselves relegated to transport, escort and patrol duties.

The Vietnamese Navy continued to grow in the ten years following the end of the Indochina War. But the Vietnamese added little to the art of brown water warfare beyond what they had learned from the French. By 1965 the Vietnamese Navy comprised a Sea Force of

2000 men, fifty American advisors, and fifty-seven ships and large craft. The River Force had grown to nine RAGs and totalled 1300 men and twenty-seven American advisors; seven of the RAGs had fourteen boats each, while the other two were equipped for heavy transport and escort duties. The third component of the navy was the newly created Coastal Force manned by some 4000 Vietnamese and over 100 American advisors. This, originally, was the paramilitary Junk Force that had been integrated into the navy and was soon to have 600 motor and sail junks to operate. Lastly, there was the Vietnamese Marine Corps Brigade of 7000 men and twenty-four U.S. Marine Corps advisors.

The systematic expansion of the Vietnamese brown water navy was matched by the intensification of the insurgency. The Vietnamese were outpaced by these events, and, in 1965, the United States entered its own combat units into the contest. Early that year the Americans had also assumed an important rôle in coastal surveillance and, shortly thereafter, took on the equally responsible task of patrolling the major inland waterways. These operations, code-named 'Market Time' and 'Game Warden', respectively, were carried on in coordination with those of the Vietnamese.

The Americans acknowledged the sovereignty of South Vietnam and conducted their operations accordingly. But, it was soon evident that all the Swift boats, coast guard cutters, radar picket escort ships, minesweepers, and patrol aircraft making up 'Market Time' forces were carrying most of the coastal surveillance burden. In similar fashion, the 200 fast fiber-glass patrol boats brought in for 'Game Warden' were the major patrol force on the inland waters. The importance of the American contribution in these two endeavors lies in the resources available and the energy with which they were utilized. This is also demonstrated by the ability of the Americans to integrate complementary equipment capabilities and coordinate operations. This quality was further evidenced in the sixty-two amphibious landings conducted from 1965 to 1969 with ships of the U.S. Seventh Fleet and troops drawn from fleet forces or those already deployed in-country.

The establishment of the Americans on the coastal and inland waters of Vietnam placed them but a step away from direct involvement in riverine warfare. This last began in 1966 with the decision to organize the Mekong Delta Mobile Afloat Force, later simply called the Mobile River Force (MRF). This organization borrowed heavily from the French but added its own innovations in due course.

From its inception the MRF was conceived of as comprising both a landing force and the boats to move, protect and support it. The French had advanced such a concept but had not been able to implement it. The Americans, however, brought the 2nd Brigade of the U.S. Army's 9th Infantry Division together with two river assault squadrons (RAS) of the U.S. Navy's River Flotilla One. Further, and as an innovation of their own, the Americans provided ships, boats and pontoons upon which to base the force afloat.

The U.S. river assault squadrons, several generations removed from the French dinassauts and the Vietnamese RAGs, had just over 100 boats. This was far more than any of their predecessors had had. However, the LCM remained as the basic craft. As the French had done, these were modified for command, fire support and troop transport functions. The American versions of these LCM were more elaborate and followed standardized patterns but their rôles were the same. Similarly, where the French had designed the STCAN/FOM patrol boat, the Americans built the assault support patrol boat (ASPB) conceived for the same rôle.

The formations used by the riverine assault forces on the waterways were like those of armored columns advancing in a conventional ground environment. The French had noted this similarity first and had devised boat modifications and operational formations accordingly. Riverine forces thus moved behind a screen of patrol boats, some of which also served as minesweepers. The landing elements that followed were protected and supported in the assault and, later, ashore by other patrol boats and monitors. The Americans applied these concepts in their own operations which, even though similar to those of the French, were on a grander scale.

The French had also used paratroop units in conjunction with river force operations. This required the coordinated actions of separate elements moving by different means and was difficult to execute successfully. The Americans did the same thing but, using helicopters, they were able to plan and execute tactical engagements of water and airborne units under more favorable conditions. The availability of large numbers of helicopters in the Vietnam War has since caused speculation over whether or not the MRF was really necessary. Since helicopters can swiftly deploy and support a force independently of the intervening terrain, why then accept an 8-knot rate of advance in clumsy vulnerable boats?

The question has merit and is well worth investigation. However, for this narrative, it suffices to record that the American forces engaged in riverine assault operations from 1967 to 1970 used helicopters with great effect for the maneuver of troops, emergency resupply and medical evacuations. The addition of a small helicopter landing platform to the armored troop carriers attests to the close relationship that existed between the MRF and its supporting helicopters.

American riverine assault operations differed from those of the French principally in scale. The dinassaut could embark only one company; the RAS could embark a two-battalion force. The French were able to spare reconnaissance and close support aircraft on infrequent occasions. The Americans had fixed and rotary-wing aviation units routinely available to cover and support riverine operations. French artillery could only support operations when the river forces were within range. The Americans devised floating platforms that enabled their artillery to accompany the riverine assault force. All these comparisions are matters of magnitude. There was, however, one major conceptual difference that gave to the American MRF a greater effectiveness; that was the matter of basing.

The French had their dinassauts based separately along the waterways. This required them to use ground units for base defense, even when the base was only temporary. French reports reveal that these arrangements were never satisfactory. Moreover, French records show that their river forces suffered greater losses among their boats when at anchor than when underway. Then, too, the small infantry units assigned to dinassauts were not intended for base defense. When they had to be used for such purposes the effectiveness of the dinassaut was impaired. The Americans, in contrast, based their river force afloat. This provided the ground troops with better amenities and greatly facilitated the servicing and maintenance of the boats. Further, the base ships, LSTs usually, had substantial firepower that lessened the need for elaborate defenses ashore. Finally, the fact that the whole base could move made it easy to shift operations from one trouble spot to another. This had already demonstrated its utility in the case of 'Game Warden' whose patrol boats were ship-based and could therefore quickly change patrol areas as circumstances required.

At the time of the French, dinassauts not engaged in combat operations were routinely used for patrolling. This placed heavy demands on men and equipment and limited operational capabilities. The Americans had a separate river patrol force, 'Game Warden', and were able to use their MRF mainly for combat operations. Moreover, they had enough boats to maintain a high operational readiness. While the magnitude of their resources was the key element in the greater capabilities of the Americans, their use of an afloat base which could move 5000 men over 200 kilometers in 24 hours and launch a strike operation within 30 minutes of anchoring further enhanced their already considerable effectiveness.

The American mobile riverine force operated for two years. It coordinated its operations with Vietnamese and other American units but otherwise generally retained its autonomy. This latter characterization applied equally well to 'Market Time' and 'Game Warden' forces whose operations were essentially independent; albeit coordinated. Then, beginning in 1968, additional naval assets started arriving in-country. These were promptly put to the task of blockading Cambodia by interdicting the inland waterways over which the communists were infiltrating troops and supplies into South Vietnam.

These blockade operations, codenamed 'Sealords', were later extended to the control of lateral communications in the delta and to the reduction of communist controlled coastal areas. Unlike other American brown water operations, 'Sealords' made use of any and all forces and depended mainly on Vietnamese units to serve as landing forces. Hence, along the coast 'Market Time' forces dominated, on the inland waters 'Game Warden' forces had important functions and throughout the delta assault operations were conducted with MRF or other more recently deployed boat units. In 1969, when the MRF ceased to exist, its assets passed to 'Sealords'. This, however, was but an interim measure, for the United States was then beginning to turn assets over to the Vietnamese so that they could take on a greater responsibility for the war. The transfer of brown water warfare assets was completed by 1970. Thereafter, the fate of the delta rested with the Vietnamese.

The first navies in history were brown water navies. They consisted of river and inshore coastal forces which sailed beyond brown waters at their peril. But, with advances in shipbuilding, propulsion and navigation, blue water navies appeared. The development of road and rail nets further contributed to the decline of brown water forces. Today, references concerned with the composition of navies usually confine themselves to sea-going ships only. Yet the record of recent history is full of examples of wars that feature important river campaigns and decisive inshore coastal actions. These, as further reading reveals, were most often fought by forces organized, trained and equipped for other purposes. The circumstances were no different in Indochina.

The French had a good start toward meeting brown water warfare requirements when they deployed their naval brigade with the first elements of the Expeditionary Corps that landed in Saigon. Even so, the brigade organization had to be modified in 1946 and again in 1947 before the dinassaut was conceived. The Americans brought in the U.S. Marines when they deployed their combat forces into the country in 1965, but these were wholly engaged in the northernmost part of South Vietnam. The U.S. Marines' brown water experience, other than that acquired through their participation in the ship-to-shore operations of the Seventh Fleet, was limited to using amphibian tractors to move and support troops operating in the restricted waterways of Annam.

Had the U.S. Marines been made available for redeployment to the Mekong delta area they would still have had to undergo specialized training to prepare them for an unfamiliar type of warfare. But at least they had amphibious experience and a long-standing working relationship with the navy. The U.S. Army did not have these attributes and the U.S. Navy had neither boats, men, nor experience in brown water warfare. Thus, all had to begin from zero; there was not even a fund of documentation that could be used to develop reliable training programs. The only experience available was that of the French and, to a lesser extent, that of the Vietnamese and the American advisors who had served in Indochina between the Indochina and Vietnam Wars.

When the Indochina War ended, the French turned over their brown water resources to the Vietnamese and departed. Fifteen years later the Americans did the same. Once again, history has been repeated and all that remains of the brown water navies of southeast Asia rests in the military archives of France and the United States, and in the hands of the Vietnamese communist government.

Index

References to illustrations are in *italic*

159